SOCIAL WORK AND POVERTY

*TO MY PARENTS AUDREY AND EDWARD DOWLING
AND MY GRANDMOTHER HILDA JACKAMAN*

Social Work and Poverty
Attitudes and actions

MONICA DOWLING
Royal Holloway, University of London

LONDON AND NEW YORK

First published 1999 by Ashgate Publishing

Reissued 2018 by Routledge
2 Park Square, Milton Park, Abingdon, Oxon, OX14 4RN
711 Third Avenue, New York, NY 10017, USA

Routledge is an imprint of the Taylor & Francis Group, an informa business

Copyright © M. Dowling 1999

All rights reserved. No part of this book may be reprinted or reproduced or utilised in any form or by any electronic, mechanical, or other means, now known or hereafter invented, including photocopying and recording, or in any information storage or retrieval system, without permission in writing from the publishers.

Notice:
Product or corporate names may be trademarks or registered trademarks, and are used only for identification and explanation without intent to infringe.

Publisher's Note
The publisher has gone to great lengths to ensure the quality of this reprint but points out that some imperfections in the original copies may be apparent.

Disclaimer
The publisher has made every effort to trace copyright holders and welcomes correspondence from those they have been unable to contact.

A Library of Congress record exists under LC control number: 99072361

ISBN 13: 978-1-138-34570-6 (hbk)
ISBN 13: 978-1-138-34572-0 (pbk)
ISBN 13: 978-0-429-43772-4 (ebk)

Contents

Figures and tables ix
Acknowledgements x
Preface xi
Foreword xiii
Alan Walker

Introduction 1

Chapter 1 - The relationship between social work and poverty 5
A definition of poverty 5
Poverty and stigma - a subjective interpretation 8
Definitions of social work 9
Definitions of welfare rights 10
The origins of the relationship between poverty and social work 11
The philosophy and practices of the Charity Organisation Society (COS) 11
Social work and psychiatry 13
The casework model 14
The income maintenance system and the functions of social services
    departments 15
Social workers as providers of income maintenance and/or as
    advocates/advisers on income maintenance matters 19
Social work and poverty today 23
Conclusions 24

Chapter 2 - The restructuring of welfare 27
What is the restructuring of welfare? 27
Social service users, social workers and the restructuring of social
    security 28

Social service users and the restructuring of the housing market	33
Conclusions	42

Chapter 3 - Methodological perspectives — 45
Relating theory and method	45
A critique	45
A discussion on the nature of subjectivity	51
A feminist methodology	53
Group discussion	55
Participant observation - a reflexive account	57
Access	58
The role of a participant observer	59
The effectiveness of the research in terms of policy and practice	61
Research feedback	61
Conclusions	64

Chapter 4 - Social work students and social work education — 66
How do social work students come to know and learn?	66
Research on social work education	68
What have we learnt so far about social work education?	69
What is professional knowledge?	70
The relationship between theory and practice	73
Conclusions	76

Chapter 5 - Social work students' attitudes to poverty — 78
Students' views on the relationship between poverty and social work	78
Social control and non intervention	82
Women and poverty	85
Social work placements	87
Students' views on the future relationship between social work and poverty	92
Overseas studies	93
A poverty awareness programme	94
Conclusions	96

Chapter 6 - Social workers' attitudes and actions in relation to poor social service users — 98
Social workers' attitudes and actions	99
Theoretical models for understanding attitudes and actions	100
Social psychological theories	100
A critique of the social psychological perspective	103

Social construction	105
Previous research on social workers' attitudes to poverty	105
Fieldwork findings	106
Observation studies	108
Team policies on Section 17 monies	114
Miss Lerner and Section 17 monies	116
Policy implications - income maintenance	117
Research findings - 'deserving' and 'undeserving' poor	118
Financial problems - deserving of social work time?	121
Research findings - welfare benefits	121
Conclusions	124

Chapter 7 - Social service users with financial difficulties - their responses — 126

Power and authority	126
Characteristics of social service users interviewed	127
Satisfactions of social service users	128
Dissatisfactions of social service users	133
Participant observation in a social services waiting room	138
How users would have liked social services to respond differently	139
Social workers' attitudes and actions in comparison to users' views	140
Life events	141
Key issues for social service users and carers	142
Conclusions	143

Chapter 8 - Social work, poverty and social exclusion — 145

Who are the users of social services who have financial difficulties and why are they poor?	145
How do social work students and social workers negotiate with social service users and why are they dealt with in the ways described and analysed?	146
Social workers and professionalism	147
A user's guide - information, guide-lines, accountability, access and participation	148
Confidentiality	150
Cash and care	150
Social exclusion	152
Government policies on poverty, social exclusion and social services	153
Community care - a redistribution of financial need?	157
Possible solutions - community care and financial need	160
Poverty awareness	162

Policy and research recommendations 164
Concluding note 165

Appendix 1 166

Appendix 2 168

Appendix 3 171

Appendix 4 178

Bibliography 180

Index 193

Figures and tables

Figure 1.1	The social work task in the 1990s - cash and/or care : the wider environment	17
Figure 1.2	Three perspectives on poverty and community care	18
Figure 1.3	Arguments for and against dealing with poverty being part of the social work task	20
Figure 1.4a	Arguments for and against 'cash' role being part of the social work task : Direct cash payments	21
Figure 1.4b	Arguments for and against 'cash' role being part of the social work task : Advice/advocacy on income maintenance	22
Figure 3.1	Method and theory integration - Methodological concerns	46
Figure 3.2	Method and theory integration - Interests	47
Figure 6.1	A social/psychological view of the relationship between attitudes and actions	104
Figure 6.2	The research findings in relation to previous research findings on social workers' attitudes to poverty	110

Acknowledgements

Firstly thanks to all the social service users, social workers, students, and social services staff who have participated in the research. Without their support and cooperation in dealing with difficult and sometimes emotional issues, this book would not have been possible.

Secondly thanks to all my colleagues at the University of Sheffield and RHBNC, University of London for their help and advice. Jan Morgan and Sheila Sweet at Royal Holloway did a great job on type setting the book for the publishers.

Finally thanks to family, friends and my husband Martin Rudd for support and care during the times of exhilaration, trauma and stress that completing this work has involved.

Preface

In 1975 I was asked by someone not connected with social work whether I thought the families with financial difficulties I was visiting for the Housing Department were different from other families. Had they not got these enormous debts because they were lazy, bad, or more stupid than other people? I could honestly answer that from my observations I did not see them as different from other families I knew. I was surprised because I had not up to then linked the social work placement I was undertaking to peoples' attitudes to 'deserving' and 'undeserving' poor, despite this being the fourth year of my social work course. The theory and practice of social work were not integrated.

The aim of this book is to investigate: social workers' attitudes and actions towards poverty issues; social service users who have needed financial help - their attitudes to social workers; and to question whether learning about poverty is an integrated part of social work students' training and social workers' in-service training.

The research is influenced not only by my own experiences of being a social work student and social worker, but also by being a social work teacher and researcher and an unemployed income support claimant in between periods of teaching and while looking for a job after periods of studying.

Being unemployed and living on benefits is an experience that has become common for undergraduate and postgraduate students if only on a temporary basis. It is common for longer periods of time for greater sections of the population in the 1980s and 90s than was the case in the 1950s, 60s or 70s. The experience is not one most people would wish to continue. However many individuals who go to social services for financial help have children or are disabled which often makes their situation far more difficult to escape. Any comparison between groups of poor claimants is difficult to maintain - however the experience of receiving money from the State and thus being part of a 'dependant' population, is understood by all who have had to live on State benefits for however short a time, and many who have not.

Foreword

The relationship between social work and poverty is close and long-standing: as long as there has been a profession of social work the vast majority of its clients have been poor and experiencing different forms of social exclusion. In this important book Monica Dowling subjects this relationship to a welcome new perspective which explores the subjective interaction between social workers and the poor and which traces the ways in which workers' attitudes and actions are influenced by their training, personal backgrounds and the wider/political economy. Monica Dowling's book is not an arid or abstract investigation, but one which is informed throughout by well researched insights into the attitudes and experiences of social service users, social workers and social work students. She presents a powerful case for the compulsory use of poverty awareness training which is as important in social work as disability, gender, race and age awareness.

This book represents a challenge to social workers to confront the material deprivation of social service users, social work educators to improve teaching about poverty and social exclusion and policy makers to abolish poverty and social exclusion.

Alan Walker
University of Sheffield

Introduction

This study has investigated to what extent social workers' attitudes to poverty have been translated into actions. It includes a consideration of the ways in which social workers aid social service users with financial difficulties - through welfare rights advice and/or advocacy or direct cash payments. Social workers are increasingly being expected to collude with the DSS's' functions of income maintenance and therefore their role as welfare rights advocates/advisers has been compromised. However social service users' increasing poverty indicates that social work help with financial and material needs may be an important part of the social work task from a consumer' perspective, both in training and in work.

Social work students had more positive attitudes than social workers towards dealing with poverty in practice, and were critical of the social control functions of social workers in relation to income maintenance. However, they were not similarly subject to the controls and norms of social work institutions. The poverty awareness programme, created as a result of the fieldwork findings, allows social workers and social work students to become more aware of conflicts between attitudes and actions, and fulfils students' needs for an understanding of poverty that integrates theory and practice.

Some social service users constructed their financial problems differently from the way social workers perceived them. However users were generally grateful for any financial help or advice they received, but tended to find such help stigmatising. Some users had turned to welfare rights agencies for further financial advice where such agencies were available.

This book is primarily concerned with the interaction of social workers with poor users of social services departments. It asks: who are the users of social services who have financial difficulties and why are they poor? How do social workers and social work students negotiate with such users and why are they dealt with in the ways described and analysed?

The aim of the study is to present a qualitative account of how social service users, social workers and social work students function in relation to issues of poverty and inequality. It is unique in that although there have been participant and nonparticipant studies of social work teams (Johnson 1975, Mattinson and Sinclair 1979, Satyamurti 1981, Smith 1980, Pithouse 1987) they have not addressed in detail the concerns of poor service users. Social work research that has focused on poverty, has concentrated on social workers' and social service users' attitudes to poverty, (Currie and Davidson 1984, Taylor 1990, Becker 1997) whereas this research examines the relationship between attitudes and actions of social workers and social service users. It suggests that there is no necessary logical progression from attitudes to actions. Although issues of welfare rights and income maintenance are addressed as ways in which social workers may tackle poverty among social service users, the study has the wider perspective of investigating how social workers' 'cash' and 'care' roles are integrated in their everyday attitudes and actions.

The study also examines the role of social work education in preparing social workers for their future occupation. Studies of social work students have tended to be quantitative rather than qualitative (Parsloe 1978, CCETSW 1988, National Institute of Social Work 1998). Although such research has considered social work students as consumers of social work education, it has not tackled the attitudes of social work students to the problem of financial need of users, nor how the policy and personal issues of the relationship between poverty and social work could be addressed in DipSW courses. As part of the fieldwork, group discussions and individual interviews on social work and poverty were conducted with postgraduate and non-graduate social work students at Sheffield University and Sheffield Hallam University.

A thirteen month participant observation study of two social work teams from 'Carshire' and 'City' local authorities is the main focus of the book although eighteen in depth interviews with social service users are also recorded and analysed. Interviews with social service users obtained their views on the interactions observed in the fieldwork setting. This methodological approach involves triangulation of attitudes and actions. However users' actions have not been observed as exhaustively as social workers' actions because the fieldwork settings were two social services departments where social workers play the dominant role.

The observation study was conducted in Carshire (with the Silverton social work team) and City (with the City social work team). Carshire is a small, rural, former mining area while 'City' is the nearby large metropolis where most of the population used to work in a single heavy industry. With the loss of this industry, 'City' is attempting to develop its service sector. In both areas there is high unemployment and poverty.

Throughout the book, names of students, social workers and social service users have been changed to protect their privacy. It was a condition of access to the social work teams that their local authority and place of work were also confidential. The team observed for nine months, three days a week are 'Silverton' and the team observed for two days a week for four months, are called the 'City' team. It was agreed prior to interviewing all social service users that information received from them would not be passed back to social workers without the user's consent.

As the aim of the book is to integrate theory with social work practice throughout, the fieldwork findings are not concentrated in one or two chapters but referred to in most chapters with more in depth analysis in chapters 4 to 7.

Chapter 1 defines the concepts of poverty, welfare rights and social work as they will be used throughout the book. This is followed by a consideration of stigma as applied to poverty in order to give meaning to attitudes and action observed during the fieldwork. The chapter then examines what sort of relationship has existed between social work, welfare rights and poverty and how this compares with the reality of the relationship today.

Chapter 2 examines the wider social policy context in which this study has taken place. It argues that a restructuring of welfare is occurring in relation to social services. Two areas of restructuring - housing and social security - are investigated with examples from the fieldwork.

Chapter 3 assesses in what ways the research has incorporated theory and method, subjectivity and objectivity, qualitative and quantitative methods and feminist methodology. It suggests that: subjectivity and its implications for qualitative methods; feedback to research respondents; suggested policy initiatives from research, and gender interactions, are areas of methodological interest that need further exploration.

Chapter 4 concentrates on social work education and the social work students' responses to the group discussion interviews. How we come to know, and how students come to know about social work is evaluated from a hermeneutic framework.

Chapter 5 discusses social work students' evaluation of the present and future relationship between social work and poverty. Results from the group discussions show how students' previous work and placement experiences affect their attitudes, and how they account for their actions. A poverty awareness programme is proposed.

Chapter 6 introduces a critique of previous research on social workers' attitudes and actions in relation to poverty. Fieldwork findings from the current participant observation research are presented and social-psychological and social constructionist theories are employed to understand the findings and the relationship between attitudes and behaviour.

Chapter 7 is concerned with the perspectives of social service users with financial difficulties. It explores their responses to individual social workers in helping with their problems and users' satisfactions, dissatisfactions and suggestions for change within social services. The findings are discussed in relation to relevant participant observation data from the fieldwork.

Chapter 8 draws together the main themes of the book, points out where further research would be valuable, defends the need for policies on poverty, social work *and* social exclusion and argues that poverty awareness programmes are one way forward.

1 The relationship between social work and poverty

This chapter defines the concepts of poverty and social work as they will be used throughout the book and traces the past and present connections between poverty and social work. It is suggested that although there is a historical, factual, objective relationship between poverty and social work, there is also a subjective interactive relationship between social workers and those in poverty which is based on professional traditions, the casework model, and social workers' own attitudes and actions. These attitudes and actions are influenced by social workers' training and personal backgrounds and the larger political environment.

Relevant to the relationship between poverty and social work, and therefore also included in this chapter are an analysis of the relationship between the income maintenance system and the functions of social services departments, and a summary of the issues concerning social workers as *providers* of income maintenance and as *advocates/advisers* on income maintenance matters.

A definition of poverty

A 'poverty line' which divides those who are poor from those who are not poor could be useful in defining what percentage of the population are poor. However there is a continuing debate about where such a 'poverty line' should be set and to what extent poverty is relative to the society in which it exists (Oppenheim and Harker 1996, Townsend 1979). There is no official UK government 'poverty line' but two sources of government information are *Low Income Families* statistics and *Households below Average Income* statistics, both derived from the *Family Expenditure Survey*. Households below average income (HBAI) statistics are the government measure of low income while 50 per cent of average income is used by CPAG, the European Community and international studies as a measure of poverty. However households are the unit of definition rather than the family or individual and such a statistic does not relate income to the minimum rates of benefit specified by Parliament. Other methods of measuring poverty and some would say inequality include: the level at which 40 per cent of the population receive less than 15 per cent of the income of the country (Todaro 1994); those spending less than half of the country's national average expenditure (EEC 1991); or the real income of the poorest fifth (Townsend 1991); or tenth of the population (Johnson and Webb 1991).

Although the government has not provided HBAI statistics by region, a number of deprivation indicators show that Northern Ireland still ranks as one of the poorest areas in terms of unemployment, income and reliance on income support. The 'North'/ 'South' divide of the 1980s appears to have become less of a divide in the 1990s with the disproportionate effect of the recession on the South East in the early 1990s (Oppenheim and Harker 1996). However Pond (1989) and Townsend (1979) and Oppenheim (1991) point out that even greater divisions in terms of income and wealth can exist within regions.

Information on women and poverty was particularly relevant to the research as many of the social service users with financial difficulties interviewed and observed were lone mothers on income support. Women from poor relief days up to the present time have always been at greater risk of poverty (Glendinning and Millar 1992). Oppenheim and Harker (1996) estimate from 1995 social security statistics that 59 per cent of adults supported by income support are women. Nine out of ten lone parents are female and 1,097,000 lone parents were reliant on income support in 1994. Over half were dependent on income support for several years and 658,000 had been on income support for two years or more (DSS 1995). As Millar and Glendinning (1992) note women's risk of poverty as compared to men's is concerned with access to income, time spent on generating income or resources and the transfer of these resources within households.

Poverty statistics give a quantitative perspective, but they do not reveal the intricacies of poor peoples' lives. Poverty can be of a temporary or long term nature (Walker 1991). It can mean that those who feel themselves to be poor are not accepted as such and that those who are on benefits and considered poor may be earning unofficially (Jordan, James, Kay and Redley 1992). Poverty may involve feelings of despair and depression which can exacerbate any financial difficulties.

Initially the definition of poverty for the purposes of this book was based on an income at or below income support levels. However income support levels are such a low level of income that few people can manage to survive on these benefits alone. This calls into question any objective definition of poverty which does not allow for human motivation, intervention, frailty or manipulation. Thus the approach to poverty used throughout the book will suggest firstly that there is no objective measure of poverty that is consistent for all times and places:

> Measuring poverty must always be relative, since what it is measuring is a social product which changes both over time and from one society to another. The point at issue simply becomes what it is relative to (Novak 1988, p.21).

Secondly that the poor are now poorer in relation to the wealthy than they were in 1979 (see Chapter 2). Thirdly, a 'poverty line' may be a necessary quantitative means for measuring poverty in the population as a whole but does not allow for the individual needs of people like Mrs Dixon (see Chapter 2) who are on the margins of poverty but do not necessarily see themselves in that way.

As Oppenheim (1990a) notes on behalf of the Child Poverty Action Group (CPAG):

> We also take account of those people living just above each of these poverty lines - those living on the margins of poverty. It is important to hold on to the idea of such a margin, since people living on low incomes usually find that their income fluctuates, slipping between poverty and an income close to poverty. We describe anyone living between 100 per cent and 140 per cent of supplementary benefit or between 50 per cent and 60 per cent of average income as living on the margins of poverty.

Balloch and Jones' (1990, p.2) study *Poverty and Anti-Poverty Strategy* defines poverty as lack of money, lack of resources and lack of control and quotes The Archbishop of Canterbury *Faith in the City* (1986):

> Poor people ... are at the mercy of fragmented and apparently unresponsive public authorities. They are trapped in housing and in environments over which they have little control. They lack the means and opportunity - which so many of us take for granted - of making choices in their lives.

Poverty and stigma - a subjective interpretation

> While the stranger is present before us, evidence can arise of his possessing an attribute that makes him different from others in the category of persons available for him to be, and of a less desirable kind - in the extreme, a person who is quite thoroughly bad, or dangerous or weak. He is thus reduced in our minds from a whole and usual person to a tainted and discounted one. Such an attribute is a stigma (Goffman 1990, p.2).

Poverty falls within the realm of 'stigma'. It is not *being* poor that is a stigma, but the social perception of the attribute which deems it a stigma. Goffman (1990, p.4) suggests three types of stigma: physical 'stigma deformities', 'tribal stigma of race, nation and religion' and 'blemishes of individual character'. Thus the poor are perceived by the non poor as having more character defects than the rich, hence the 'culture of poverty' thesis. Stigmatising the poor has cultural, political and historical traditions which cannot be easily avoided by the individual (Novak 1988, Waxman 1988, Dean 1991).

Poverty can be understood as a special type of stigma which attributes to the poor a status of being less than human. It has taken various forms at different historical stages: branding in the fourteenth century (De Schweinitz 1961, Pound 1973); being driven into workhouses in the nineteenth century (Novak 1988, Waxman 1988) and being labelled as part of 'the underclass' and treated accordingly in the late twentieth century (Murray 1990).

Blaming and stigmatising the poor is convenient for the more well off for it absolves them from any moral responsibility towards solving the problem of poverty. Galbraith (1996) indicates that the latest punitive welfare reforms in the US are the result of the majority of the population who are working and solvent, no longer caring about the plight of the poor. As Waxman (1983, p.69) comments,

> The sociological study of poverty and the poor should include, it is argued, not only the behaviour of the poor themselves, but also the nature of the relationship between the poor and the non poor, specifically the perceptions and the definitions the non poor have of the poor...

At any particular time in any society, each individual will have their own preconceptions of what constitutes poverty. Most people have an un-thought out emotional response as to whether an individual measures up to their own internal view of what a poor person should be like. In the same way we might have an immediate feeling of 'inappropriateness' if we see a black/female/older/ disabled person in a situation where we are not expecting to see such a person, so a person we define as poor who has a good standard of decoration in their house, a computer or a car may evoke a similar response. Prejudging takes place continuously, which helps us to make sense of the world in some situations, for example if someone is coming towards us holding a knife in a threatening manner. However the ease with which prejudgements are made about the poor is why poverty awareness is just as important as disability, gender, race or age awareness.

The subjective nature of poverty and its relationship to stigma suggests that objective measures only partially explain the phenomena. They do not explain the interactive effect of individuals on each other which can affect micro and macro policy outcomes.

Definitions of social work

Some social workers in the fieldwork defined social work as the casework relationship, some students saw social work as 'sticking plaster - we act as sticking plaster without actually tackling and doing something'. Social service users talked about caring people or busybodies. Generally there was confusion and uncertainty among all three researched groups about what social work was, whether social workers were actually doing social work and if not, what they should be doing instead.

Quantitative responses to the first national opinion survey into attitudes towards social workers appeared to show the public as less muddled than those more intimately involved with social work. Forty three per cent of 994 respondents replied (broadly) that they helped people in need of help, 37 per cent that they advised on and sorted out people's problems, and 3 per cent saw them as 'busybodies' or 'interfering people'. When people were asked what social workers should do as part of their job, about three quarters said that social workers should investigate the needs of disabled people and 64 per cent that they should help poor people get their rights. Helping people with their emotional needs ranked third (54 per cent) and statutory tasks a poor fourth (32.5 per cent). However the public did not appear to see personal social services as a service appropriate for all sections of the population - only 8 per cent of the 994 respondents interviewed, had discussed a problem with a social worker compared to 12 per cent for CAB workers and doctors who were top with 29 per cent (Gallup 1981).

Some authors have argued that social work is a particularly subjective and individualistic type of work which is prone to different interpretations while Pincus and Minahan (1977, p.43) define the *purpose* of social work as:

(1) to enhance the problem solving and coping capacities of people; (2) to link people with systems that provide them with resources, services and opportunities; (3) to promote the effective and human operation of these systems; and (4) to contribute to the development and improvement of social policy.

CCETSW, the body that regulates social work training, has defined social work as

> ...an accountable professional activity which enables individuals, families and groups to identify personal, social and environmental difficulties adversely affecting them. Social work enables them to manage these difficulties through supportive rehabilitative, protective or corrective action. Social work promotes social welfare and responds to wider social needs promoting equal opportunities for every age, gender, sexual preference, class, disability, race, culture and creed. Social work has the responsibility to protect the vulnerable and exercise authority under statute (CCETSW 1991, p.8).

These definitions would appear to allow ample opportunities for social workers to be supportive of individuals with financial difficulties. However there is a longstanding debate concerning *how much* of the professional role of the social worker should be concerned with alleviating poverty. Although there is evidence to link poverty and social work traditionally and theoretically, the connections between poverty and social work are also subjective, ambiguous and complex.

Definitions of welfare rights

'Welfare rights' has been used to describe a wide range of activities as well as a set of ideas. Holman (1973a, p.358) defines the concept quite narrowly as being 'the entitlement of low income persons to statutory, financial or material provision of services', whereas Cohen and Rushton (1982, p.1) widen it to include the *action* of advocacy which they define as 'acting on a client's behalf and representing her interests to outside organisations'. For the purpose of this study I wish to borrow Fimister's (1986, p.1) definition of welfare rights as being:

> ... rights to income, with particular reference to social security and other cash welfare benefits, and to directly related issues such as fuel disconnections.

Within this definition Fimister includes advocating for people's rights, being concerned with the relief of poverty and also the prevention of poverty through campaigning for 'clear, adequate and enforceable non-means-tested entitlements'.

In relation to social work, the CCETSW Curriculum Development Group on Welfare Rights in Social Work Education notes (1989, p.8) 'Welfare rights for social workers is regarded as an orientation to helping and a practice skill rather than a body of knowledge'. However, welfare rights is an important skill that appears neglected in social work training and in practice (Becker 1997).

The origins of the relationship between poverty and social work

The relationship between social work and poverty appears to have been influenced by three main factors: the philosophy and practises of the Charity Organisation Society (COS); the need for an emerging profession to identify with other more powerful professions, in this case psychiatry, and the administrative and bureaucratic development of the casework model. The history and origins of social work are crucial in understanding the training, attitudes and actions of social workers today, in relation to poverty issues.

The roots of social work lie in a nineteenth century world of philanthropy and discretion. This was a society in which caseworkers and Poor Law officials investigated the circumstances of poor people in order to decide whether they deserved access to welfare goods and services provided by the state and charitable organisations. However, these activities were not just directed at separating the deserving from the undeserving, they were also concerned with moral regeneration. When help was provided it was on condition that recipients improved themselves. As Stewart (1989, p.9) notes, 'Increased thrift, sobriety, personal and family discipline, were the price demanded of the recipients of Victorian welfare'.

The philosophy and practices of the Charity Organisation Society (COS)

Waxman (1988) describes in some detail the COS established in 1869, as the acknowledged forerunner of the social work profession. By emphasizing their expertise in the 'science' of helping, they were able to impose their ideology on middle class charitable individuals and the government of the day. They were concerned with the 'deserving' poor who could be reformed, rather than the 'undeserving'.

The Society (COS) operated under the assumption there *were* deserving and undeserving poor, and though it couldn't arrive at any steadfast formula for distinguishing between the two categories and finally left it at 'not likely to benefit' in place of 'undeserving'. The COS stressed the value of treating each case separately and keeping a record and raising funds for each case individually. It is from these beginnings that the casework approach to social work with its stress on the interview, home visit and assessment evolved (Waxman 1988, p.85).

This ideology of poverty was not new or held only by the COS. Novak (1988) cites the Fabian society as also having reforming or punitive views of the poor at that time and Dean (1991, p.219), suggests that this was a common view which extended to public health and factory inspectors as well as the COS.

> Each intervention from the field of philanthropy to the public health measures, would be conceived as a moralizing one, monitoring and attempting to transform the minute details of the domestic lives of the poor. If the first circle of liberal governance drew upon the workhouse to enforce wage labour, and the older semio technique of less eligibility, its second turn would increasingly find the need for a network of measures which sought actively to encourage the ethic of personal responsibility and to target women as agents.

The individualising of poverty and the stigmatising of the 'undeserving' poor was to find its most consistent champion however in the COS. Their attempt to transform charity from its semi-feudal connotations to an effective and efficient means of social control, was not wholly successful in that its procedures of investigation and moral classification met with profound hostility within the working class. As a school of social reformers, its influence on social policy extended to the domination of the 1909 Poor Law Commission whose Distress Committees were given strict instructions of procedure to follow to test the character of applicants. According to Beveridge (1909, p.24):

> The original 'Record Paper' drawn up by the Local Government Board contained eighteen paragraphs including at least fifty different questions to be asked of and answered by every applicant, together with six or more paragraphs for information to be answered after subsequent inquiry. The answers to the most important questions were directed to be verified by reference to independent sources of information.

In the words of Keir Hardie, 'every line had COS stamped across its face' (cited Harris 1972, p.174). The Distress Committees procedures alienated the 'deserving poor' they had intended to reach. Although the COS attempted to solve unemployment and poverty through individual example and voluntary effort they were overtaken by the more direct intervention of the state

(Beveridge 1942). However Novak (1988, p.99) points out that their influence '... established a tradition, philosophy and practice that was subsequently to form the basis for the contemporary practice of social work'. In this context, some social workers' practices in the fieldwork, such as giving out: cash, food parcels, food vouchers, second hand clothes, shoes and furniture, have barely changed since COS times.

Social work and psychiatry

Conceptions of counselling taught in social work training have emphasised that the individual should not be stigmatised, blamed or even given directive help (Biesteck 1961) when coming to social services. This is in opposition to COS judgements concerning deserving and undeserving poor. Theories of psychiatry, which increased social work's status as akin to medicine and were therefore seen as valuable, have however tended to stigmatise poor users of social services.

> Together with the political and social climate of individualism the psychiatric approach to casework gave further substance to the stigma theory which perceived poverty as a 'blemish of individual character' because it gave 'scientific' validation to the perception of poverty as being totally rooted in the individual to the exclusion of any possibility of environmental influences (Waxman 1988, p.89).

There is confirmation from the fieldwork, particularly in the Carshire authority, that psychiatric theories continue to be justifications for not helping people with money problems. The need for money from this perspective is merely a 'presenting' problem and hides feelings of dependence on the social worker. To give clients money is to increase that dependence. As a social work student wrote in response to a question on the role of supplementary benefits in social work:

> Student: I feel basically it's the ethos of professional social work that refuses to recognize that inadequate income is the power-house of many social problems, ...social work translates into personal, cultural deficiencies (Dowling 1986, p.23).

The CCETSW Curriculum Development Group on Welfare Rights (Stewart 1989, p.7) are concerned about this interpretation of users' problems:

> Dismissal of clients' material problems and automatic reinterpretation

of the 'presenting' problem (about money, work, housing) in terms of a 'real' problem, is paternalistic. It is contrary to the principles about respecting clients' views and rights to self determination which social workers have come to hold important.

The casework model

To recognize poverty as a character fault rather than the fault of God, cultural and/or biological inheritance or a capitalist society, meant there was room for individual improvement. Personal reform was the primary aim of COS workers and to some extent, still is for social workers using the casework model.

> By the turn of the twentieth century, while it has moved from the narrow confines of charity to a whole set of principles and techniques accompanying a social philosophy, social casework still retained many of the individualistic principles from which it was born, that is, 'a set of assumptions about the nature of human society and its organisation which belonged to the nineteenth century rather than the twentieth' (Woodroofe 1966 cited in Waxman 1988, p.87).

Social work was organised nationally and locally to combat poverty. It was in this area that members of COS professed expertise and from this area of work that the casework model developed. If poverty had been understood as having structural causes then individual casework would not have been appropriate. As it was, individual counselling to reform the person who had unfortunate personality defects was thought the best way to 'cure' poverty.

The organisation of social work, inherited from COS but developed by social reformers, academics, administrators and legislators has not allowed a structural understanding of poverty to be followed through by working with groups of users, for example, setting up self help groups such as claimants unions. In the Silverton team, two social workers had to give up their welfare rights work with older people in a local health clinic because of the demands of their casework. There was a commitment to a local 'patch' way of working in the City team, which is a step away from casework and towards community work, but this was not supported by other social work teams or given status in the authority's reorganisation policies towards specialisms. Although there are legal, statistical, and bureaucratic reasons for social work using a casework construction, tradition has been the strongest influence in maintaining a system that purports to respond to emotional and material *individual* need.

The income maintenance system and the functions of social services departments

The abolition of the Poor Law, while leaving some income related problems with local authorities, freed the embryonic social work profession from responsibilities for income maintenance administration. The separation of 'cash' from 'care' duties did however involve difficulties for Social Service Departments. They were concerned with help for families but had to distinguish between material and non-material problems when there was no clear dividing line between them. The same issue presented itself to social security officers who were charged with only meeting material needs. Stevenson (1973, p.29-30) describes this dilemma in terms of 'the interaction of the different aspects of human need - material, social and psychological'. She continues:

> Social work is, by definition, concerned with these interactions and this concern gives it its distinctive character. To concentrate on any one to the exclusion of any other is to do violence to the person in need and collude with those processes of fragmentation that are increasingly recognized as constituting a serious problem in complex urban societies.

In the 1950s and 60s social work in what were then the Children's Departments increasingly focussed on preventative work designed to support children in their own homes. Social workers became more and more dissatisfied that they could not make cash payments themselves (Packman 1975). In 1963 the Children and Young Persons Act was passed which altered this situation (slightly different later legislation had a similar impact in Scotland) by enabling local authorities to provide 'advice, guidance and assistance' to promote the welfare of children by diminishing the need to put them in care. The assistance could be 'in kind, or in exceptional circumstances, in cash'. When the Children's Departments were integrated into the more comprehensive social services departments in 1970 they took this power with them. Subsequent Children's Acts of 1980 and 1989 carried the power forward in the legislation.

Although these money giving powers were intended to give help where central government was explicitly unable to provide benefits, a number of research studies (Hill and Laing 1979, Lister and Emmett 1976, Valencia and Jackson 1979, Stewart and Stewart 1986) have indicated that these powers have taken some of the pressure off the central means-tested scheme by making payments in situations in which the DSS could have been considered responsible. Furthermore the 1986 Social Security Act has created a much more rigid Income Support system so that responses to exceptional and emergency situations are generally in the form of a loan through the cash limited Social Fund. This puts extra pressure on the small Section 17 (formerly Section

1) budgets provided by social services departments, who do not want to find that budgets have to grow rapidly to meet needs the DSS is now unprepared to meet (Jones, 1989).

The position of social service departments is further complicated by assumptions made by the DSS (and embodied in the Social Fund guidelines for their staff) that social workers will cooperate in the assessment of need for Social Fund help, particularly in sorting out cases where community care grants will help people to leave, or remain out of, institutional care. Initially the local authority associations, the main social workers' organisation (BASW) and the principal local government trade union (NALGO now UNISON) all refused to accept the role the DSS had identified for social services departments. A complicated policy of 'determined advocacy' was adopted which involved agreeing to help clients fight the Social Fund for the best possible deal (Community Care Grants being the ideal) whilst not cooperating with the Social Fund to vet claims, sort out budgeting problems or weed out 'undeserving' claimants. This was the position adopted by the City team in the fieldwork. Other social services departments such as 'Carshire' which included the Silverton team, adopted a policy of 'non co-operation' to show their antipathy to being involved in the income maintenance functions of the DSS at all.

As social security policies eliminated what claimants used to be able to claim from the DSS as of right, many claimants were approaching social services for income maintenance under Section 17 of the Children Act 1989 (formerly Section 1 of the Children's Act 1963 and 1980). In both of the social work teams observed, social workers were coming under increasing pressure, especially on the duty desk, to deal with users' financial problems that would have previously been dealt with by the local social security office.

However some parts of their work in relation to income maintenance had not changed. Social workers in both teams were involved in one off money payments which had always been part of their work (Satyamurti 1981). They liaised with DSS where users wanted advice about what benefits they could claim from DSS, or where a user was experiencing delays in payment of benefit from DSS and wanted support from a social worker (Packman 1975).

Fig 1.1 shows how the cash and care roles of SSD and DSS interact. Influences in the wider environment which will affect these interactions include: further restructuring of welfare; increasing poverty and unemployment (Oppenheim and Harker 1996) and no minimum income level (Leaper 1988); and that the majority of social service users will continue to be poor (Becker 1997).

The functions of Social Services Departments are not solely concerned with material aid. However in discussing the relationship between the income maintenance system (DSS) and the functions of social services (SSD), what has been considered is where and in what ways the two departments' responsibilities

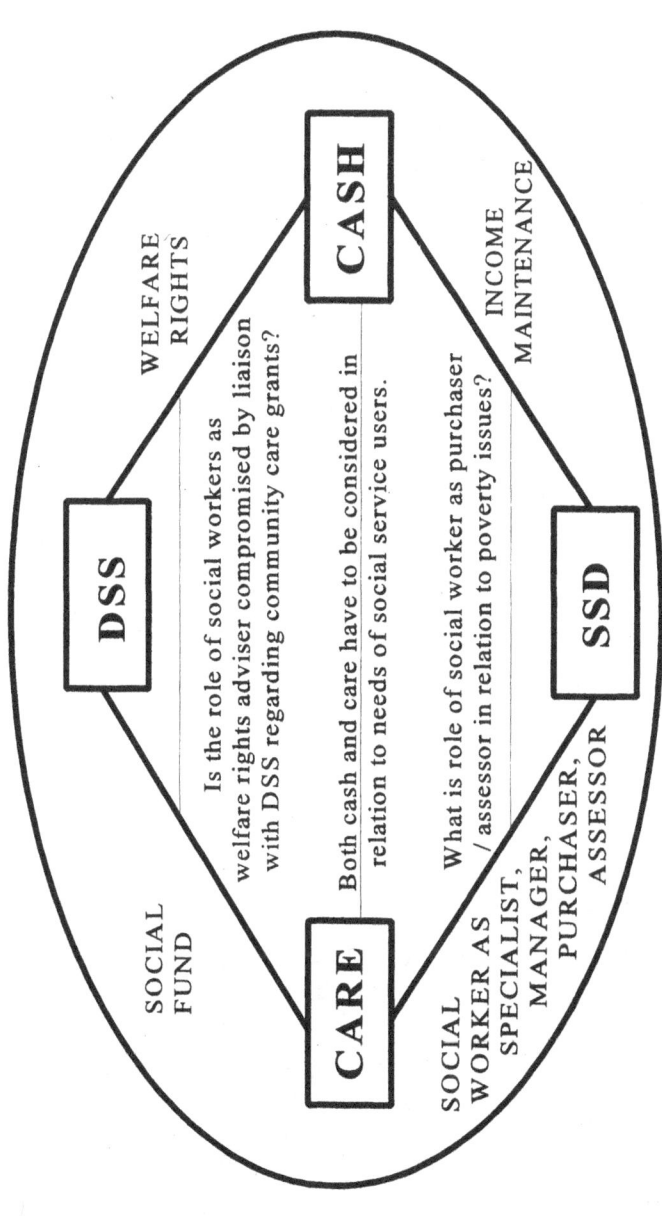

Figure 1.1 The social work task in the 1990s - cash and/or care : the wider environment

STATISTICAL PERSPECTIVE	MANAGEMENT PERSPECTIVE	EMPOWERMENT PERSPECTIVE
The numbers of claimants who are *community care users* are not sufficiently known. Estimates of nine out of 10 social service users who are claimants (Becker 1997) may not allow for new users of community care services who could not be considered poor (Drakeford 1998).	Payments for home based care if based on a nationally recognised system which is seen as equitable by all those involved, could be understood as providing a redistributive service. Money received from those who can afford to pay can be channelled back to those who cannot afford to pay for services.	Direct payments allow community care users to: take financial control over their own lives; promote independence in living in the community.

From a social services perspective direct payments could present opportunities to aid with both cash and care issues. Social workers and care managers could establish stronger links with the community through self help groups such as credit unions and debt redemption work, LETS schemes, self build initiatives, and cooperative employment arrangements. |
| However community care plans have generated quantitative information on community care users and carers and could be developed to map the extent of financial deprivation. Such information could be gathered at the assessment stage or records concerning payments for care could be collated and analysed. | However charges for home care can distort demand, deterring poor people who need home care from applying for it. Poorer localities will be unable to generate income in this way. Will poor users who cost the most money to purchasers get a worse service? As social services charge for services, will a two-tier system result where the better off buy from the private sector while social services will focus services solely on the poor?

Has the impact of community care been to push costs onto users and carers? | However involvement in direct payments can mean that social workers become judge and jury about who should and who should not receive them. Are social services being further drawn into income maintenance matters which should be the responsibility of DSS? |

Figure 1.2 Three perspectives on poverty and community care

were originally separated (Hill 1990), but have increasingly overlapped (Stewart and Stewart 1986), and how the 'cash' functions of DSS may be combined with the 'care' functions of SSD in the future (Alcock et al 1991b).

Comparative examples suggest that in some countries the cash and care roles of social workers have not been split and a more integrated approach has been possible. (Cochrane and Clarke 1993).

Social workers as providers of income maintenance and/or as advocates/advisers on income maintenance matters

There has been a continuing debate within and outside social work as to *how* social workers should aid those with financial difficulties (see Figure 1.2 and Figures 1.3a and 1.3b). Within social services departments, and providing an acknowledgement that clients' problems are complicated and exacerbated by poverty, there has developed a group of workers dealing with welfare rights. They are often social workers who have wanted to concentrate on the financial problems of social service users which other social workers have felt 'gets in the way of real social work'. The first welfare rights worker to be formally appointed within the state system was employed by Manchester Social Services Department in 1972. The appointment marked the beginning of an alternative advocacy approach by social services to the problems caused by their clients' poverty and was championed as a weapon in the new armoury of the 1970's 'radical' social worker (Cannan 1975).

Not all welfare rights posts were a development from social services work, in fact Alcock et al (1991b) and Stewart (1989) describe welfare rights work as an expansion of the neighbourhood based work of the Community Development Projects (CDP) initially in the US and later in Britain in the 60's and early 70's. Local welfare rights officers often provided an alternative less stigmatising source of support for social service users with financial problems than the social worker. Welfare rights officers have however been criticized firstly for adopting the same kind of individual casework based approach for which mainstream social work had been criticized, and secondly for in general developing outside social work teams and away from social services departments.

In the two social services departments studied, welfare rights services did not appear well integrated into the services offered by the social work teams. Welfare rights officers seemed to have limited day to day contact with social workers in Silverton and City teams. There also appeared to have been little discussion and consensus between these two groups of workers as to their policies regarding social security changes such as the Social Fund (see Chapter 2).

FOR	AGAINST
• Recent studies have clarified the link between mental and physical health and poverty and therefore dealing with users' financial problems can be preventative in terms of further casework or community care (Hannam 1988).	• Social Workers cannot respond on an individual casework basis to the structural problems of poverty.
• It is not possible to separate out completely emotional from material need (Stewart and Stewart 1991).	• For the link between cash and care to be effective, there must be a commonly accepted minimum income for all, subject to clear and simple conditions of entitlement. This is beyond the remit of social workers.
• People are forced to social services because of material need and practical problems, social workers' should therefore build up and mobilise a practical expertise.	• Social Workers cannot be expected to respond to users' increasing financial need when the government, chief officers and team managers expect social workers to cope with increasing statutory work (Langan 1993). 'Too much is generally expected of social workers' (Barclay 1982) - are they 'Jill of all trades, mistresses of none?' (Wilson 1988).
• Establishes rapport between social worker and user because users see material aid as important.	• Social Workers are not encouraged to deal with issues of poverty and welfare rights in their training nor are they encouraged by their managers and team leaders to update their knowledge when in practice.

Figure 1.3 Arguments for and against dealing with poverty being part of the social work task

Direct cash payments - S17 1989 Children's Act (income maintenance)	
For	Against
1. Use of social workers' professional judgement necessary due to restriction of social security budget (i.e. 'Better than nothing' for claimants/clients).	1. Subjective and stigmatising way of maintaining users income - back to COS origins of social work - moralistic socially controlling decisions on who is 'deserving' of cash payments and who is not.
2. Community Care grants from the social fund may be transferred to local authorities from DSS (Alcock 1991). Social workers need to work out an entitlement system or rule book that is fair for social service users and supports individual social workers.	2. Dependent on individual social workers or team leader's view of material need - idiosyncratic.
3. Crisis help mainly available as a loan from DSS.	3. Haphazard - dependent on priorities of differing social services' budgets and local authority resources.
4. Response to clients' material needs.	4. Short term relief of poverty.
5. Social work is necessarily selective. When the scale rate and operation of the benefits system are clearly not adequate, it seems unreasonable for social workers to withhold extra payments if they are able to give them (Stewart and Stewart 1986)	5. Encourages claimants who are not clients to become involved with SSD.

Figure 1.4a Arguments for and against 'cash' role being part of the social work task : Direct cash payments

| Advice/Advocacy on income maintenance (Welfare Rights) ||
For	Against
1. Welfare rights based on DSS entitlement and citizens rights, social worker in a purely advisory role.	1. Officially the job of DSS or Welfare Rights workers within the SSD.
2. Long term benefit for user if entitlement can be challenged or is calculated incorrectly.	2. When DSS benefits are restricted, little in terms of advocacy can be achieved, apart from basic benefits check.
3. Where social worker skilled and knowledgeable in welfare rights, can be satisfying part of work.	3. Social workers have variable content in their DipSW courses in poverty awareness and welfare rights and very little in service training, therefore no confidence to practice welfare rights.
4. Social Services useful base for welfare rights provision because departments are in touch with individuals with low incomes through provision of services such as Home Care, day centres and nurseries, registration of people with a handicap for car badges and aids and adaptions.	4. Welfare rights is not part of the counselling casework tradition or the new style professional social worker as a manager/purchaser of care (Clarke 1993).
5. Even the most progressive local authorities are unlikely to employ more than one Welfare Rights Officer for every 50 social service workers (Hannam 1988).	5. Welfare rights is time consuming and needs expert knowledge. Social workers may advise incorrectly therefore creating inconvenience and loss of money for social service user and more work for Welfare Rights Advisers.

Figure 1.4b Arguments for and against 'cash' role being part of the social work task : Advice/advocacy on income maintenance

The 1986 Social Security Act has left less room for manoeuvring on benefit rules, and what were extra entitlements, which some social workers and welfare rights workers have helped users apply for, have been replaced by the Social Fund. Social workers are expected to cooperate with the DSS in deciding who is 'deserving' of a grant rather than a loan. At the same time continuing high unemployment and increases in poverty amongst the unemployed, one parent families, disabled and older people (Oppenheim and Harker 1996) have meant more and more individuals are turning to social services for financial help. There is often nowhere for social workers to go for financial aid apart from Section 17(1) monies or charities.

There no longer seems a principled stand that social workers can take on *either* welfare rights (preferable for radical social workers) *or* income maintenance. Social workers are expected to be *part* of the income maintenance system in relation to community care grants. Their position on welfare rights may become compromised as they can no longer be independent experts outside the DSS system.

Alcock et al (1991b) ask the question, 'Which way for welfare rights?' and this is also a question that needs to be asked of social work in relation to poverty issues. Chapter 8 discusses for example how agendas for community care are affecting work with poor social service users.

Social work and poverty today

Policy developments in the 1980s and 90s have changed the idea of social workers reforming or supervising individuals. The new view is of social workers organising voluntary and private contractors of care while ensuring that the needs of consumers of social care are met. Social workers are generally managers of care, rather than professionals with expertise in psychology and psychiatry.

> The real significance of privatisation is the challenge it offers to traditional management and professional practices in the state welfare system...In both the health and social services after 1983, after Griffiths and the setting up of the Audit Commission, the emphasis was on objectives. New systems of management may fail to be implemented in a coherent manner yet they carry important signals to all staff and especially to those seeking to gain access to controlling positions (Kelly 1991, p.132 & 135).

The pluralist approach to social services with its emphasis on: internal markets; value for money; rationing resources by effectiveness criteria; performance indicators; purchasing, planning and quality control; and providing only essential services that cannot be contracted out; appears to offer little in terms of dealing with the growing problem of poverty. However positive outcomes could include:

- that social workers conduct basic benefits checks as part of community care assessments
- that social workers and their managers in understanding users and carers as consumers of services will appreciate how important material and practical help is to them
- that voluntary, independent and private welfare organisations support users in maximizing their income as part of their contracted out service
- that direct payments can become a viable option for larger numbers of users and carers

Kelly (1991 p.139) suggests that as the purchasing and provision of welfare are separate, those responsible for meeting need will be able to make clearer choices.

> Welfare managers have responsibilities for the professional staff they manage and the local population whose needs they are required to meet (Liddell 1989, p.58). A consequence of this is that those who control and manage services are thus faced with conflicting loyalties/expectations and may resolve these by allying themselves with the providers against the state's interest in reducing expenditure and against the consumer's demand for more and better services.

Caring for People (DOH 1989) has restructured social services, but it has not solved the problems of poverty and inequality. If as some commentators suggest, it is a smoke-screen for spending less on social services, or for redistributing resources from users to managers and management training, social service users may find they have even less help with financial problems.

Conclusions

The agency processes by which clients are evaluated in moral terms and subsequently condemned to inferior treatment must be eradicated. Only when such persons are protected against poverty discrimination (just as black people need protection against racial discrimination) can the tendency of social services to promote social deprivation be said to be in check (Holman 1973a, p.31)

If social workers are not to contribute to deepening social inequalities, they need to be aware of selection, delivery and rationing systems that can operate against the poor (Becker 1991). They need to enable the poor to learn for themselves how to handle the DSS in the same way that higher income groups have advisers to help them deal with the tax system (Cook 1989). They also need to encourage poor people to perceive their condition as the result of societal forces rather than individual inadequacies. Otherwise social workers will be contributing to the re-emergence of stigma as a deterrent to claiming benefits, which some commentators on the Social Fund see as a deliberate social policy initiative (Timmins 1988).

Social work and social work training need to change in response to consumers' demands and government directives. This can be a positive force if change is organised from within social services in partnership with social service users (Lister and Beresford 1991, International movement ATD Fourth world 1991, Morris 1994). Changes from without, imposed by government policies, with no consultation or liaison with social workers or users, are less likely to be successful.

The relationship between poverty and social work is complicated, ambiguous, and tortuous. It is not merely a relationship based on objective facts, but is concerned with ideologies, attitudes and practices relevant to social work and separately relevant to poverty. It is a subjective, interactive and dynamic relationship that will change from time to time and place to place. It is similar to any subjective relationship, the dynamics are often contradictory, conflict ridden and changeable, and are influenced by many external factors not obviously relevant to the relationship. It is neither a relationship based solely on money, nor a relationship based solely on emotional support.

It is assumed that many social problems social workers deal with could be solved if social service users and their carers had an adequate income. If everyone had enough money to live on, would we still need social workers? For survivors of disasters, children affected by incest, violence or drug abuse, social workers may still be an important resource - but only if social services are defined as the fifth social service (Townsend 1970) to which everyone in the community could turn, not just the poor.

To reverse the earlier question, if no-one had enough to live on, would we still need social workers? Probably yes, but the structural nature of poverty and the reforms or revolution needed to eradicate deprivation would become clearer (Dominelli 1988). Welfare rights, community work and countries where there is no casework model (Munday 1989), suggest social work can be preventative - by ensuring individuals are claiming the state benefits they are entitled to or enabling individuals to come together in groups to challenge the status quo and develop their own forms of social care.

The relationship between poverty and social work cannot be defined as a causal relationship, poverty does not 'cause' social work nor do most commentators think that social work 'causes' poverty. But how contingent is the relationship between the two concepts of poverty and social work? As poverty increases, does the need for social workers? If there were more social workers, would problems associated with poverty decrease?

This study explores the social construction of the relationship between social work and poverty not in an abstract society, but by understanding: the reality of working in a busy social services department; the reality of being a social work student; and the reality of being a social service user.

2 The restructuring of welfare

This chapter sets thirteen months participant observation of two social work teams and eighteen independent interviews with social service users in the wider context of government policies towards public welfare and those in poverty. It examines how welfare restructuring affects social services departments; social service users; and the interactions between social service users and social workers.

The questions addressed are, in what ways has

1. the restriction of universal benefits in favour of means tested loans and grants;
2. and the subsidising of private mortgages rather than council housing;

exacerbated the difficulties faced by poor social service users and social workers.

The research has employed an ethnographic approach to examine the policy outcomes of these forms of welfare restructuring given that the 'meaning' of government policies for the individual cannot be understood only by looking at statistics on welfare spending, changes in income tax for the wealthy, or even the increasing numbers in poverty.

What is the restructuring of welfare?

Government policies which have brought about a restructuring of welfare include: limiting public spending whilst simultaneously encouraging the private sector to respond to the unmet need; increasing the gap between rich and poor by shifting away from progressive taxation; allowing rises in market incomes whilst cutting the value of benefits in real terms; subsidising private pensions and mortgages; and limiting universal benefits in favour of means tested grants and loans.

Walker (1990a) and Shirley (1990) note that welfare state restructuring has taken place alongside rising need and inflation and has involved:

> the substitution of voluntary and private welfare for public provision; increasing the role of the informal sector in care; ... and centralisation of resource control coupled with the decentralisation of operational responsibility, thereby neutralizing any potential power of welfare state users to increase the share of public expenditure devoted to them (Walker 1990, p.33).

Regardless of policies pursued prior to 1979, (Mishra 1984, Alcock 1991a) the Thatcher Government explicitly set out to restructure welfare because it had very clear ideas about the sort of society it wanted to create - one based on enterprise rather than welfare. Successive Conservative governments assumed that if welfare aims were sacrificed for the goals of economic growth, entrepreneurs' profits would 'trickle down' to benefit the poor. After seventeen years of such policies, the evidence (Mack and Lansley 1985, Piachaud 1987, Bradshaw and Holmes 1989, Bryson 1991, 1989b, Oppenheim and Harker 1996) indicates that not only have profits not trickled down to the poor, but the poor are now poorer and the rich richer (Walker and Walker 1997).

Social service users, social workers and the restructuring of social security

What has the restructuring of social security since 1979 meant for the majority of social service users, those who are claiming benefits?

The two Social Security Acts passed in 1980 by the incoming Conservative government explicitly severed the link between long term benefits up ratings and wages, thus keeping uprating amounts to a minimum by linking them to the movement in prices. This Government also made it clear that they were happy to see the value of Child Benefit as a universal benefit eroded and between 1987 and 1990 it was frozen at £7.25 a week. The increases in Child Benefit in April and October 1991 have still meant a loss in real terms of 4 per cent since 1979 for eldest children and 22 per cent for all other children (Oppenheim and Harker 1996). The Conservative government's total saving in 1995/6 from not uprating child benefit in line with prices since 1979, and changing its structure amounts to £900 million gross and £650 million net (Oppenheim and

Harker 1996). However from April 1999, the Labour government is increasing child benefit by £2.50 a week *above* inflation for the first child - a 20 per cent increase. The poorest 20 per cent of families with children will gain an average of £500 a year from the 1998 Budget either through the Working Families Tax Credit (WFTC) or additional allowances of £2.50 a week for each child under 11.

The Social Fund

Under the previous Social Security Act (1980), **single payments for essential items such as cookers or beds had been reorganised to limit demand.** However single payments continued to increase from one million in 1981/2 to five and a half million in 1985/6. So the Social Fund which was introduced under the 1986 Social security Act and implemented in April 1988, replaced single payments with a loan scheme (70 per cent of Social Fund finance) and with a small number of grants (30 per cent of Social Fund finance) for those re-establishing themselves or wanting to stay in the community. The Labour government appears to have no plans to abolish the Social Fund and reestablish single payments for those on income support.

The participant observation part of this study was able to monitor the progress of policies in relation to the Social Fund. Mrs Dixon's situation from the Silverton area illustrates the difficulties for social service users. This lone parent is representative of other social service users interviewed and observed, who found themselves in increasingly desperate financial straits, which had an adverse effect on their mental and physical health.

Mrs Dixon

Mrs Dixon had experienced financial difficulties since her partner, a miner, had died suddenly on his first week back to work after the miner's strike. Her gas had been disconnected because of an administrative error for non payment of a £0.72 bill. Her budget plan application and normal gas bill had come through a week after she was disconnected. She had been without gas for nine to ten months. The gas reconnection charge was £80, a figure in excess of the gas charges. Moreover, she had bought a gas cooker because,

> ...it was cheaper than electric - I had no gas but a gas cooker. I couldn't feed Mary (her daughter) - she was six years old then.

Although Brian, (the welfare rights officer), John (one of the Silverton social workers), the CAB and a solicitor argued on her behalf, the Gas Board refused to reconnect without the charge being paid. These problems coupled with her sudden bereavement, sent Mrs Dixon 'over the top'. She had a breakdown and was in hospital for three months. While in hospital, her son managed to blow up the electric meter so that when she came out of hospital she was faced with the prospect of using her deceased partner's back pension award to pay for the damaged meter and the reconnection charge. She refused to pay for the gas reconnection.

> Mrs Dixon: It's the principle of the thing - I got settled without it. At that time I was fed up with being pushed about...the time in hospital hardened me...Why should I pay the gas board?...I got an electric cooker and everything, though I hadn't finished paying for the gas cooker.

Mrs Dixon had to take out a Social Fund loan to pay for an electric cooker at £7 a week out of a weekly income of £37. As a result, she had been unable to pay the Council tax. (Claimants were expected to pay 20 per cent of the Council tax after the implementation of the Social Security Act in April 1988). She had received a letter to say the bailiffs were coming to repossess her furniture because of the non payment Although she had appeared lively and cheerful when I had interviewed her three months previously, she now had an expressionless face and voice and appeared depressed.

> I've spent five to six years of my life facing authorities and getting into trouble - it's not funny you know.

John (her social worker of three years standing) had left, so Tony (who was the duty social worker when she approached social services on this occasion), phoned the department responsible for the Council tax who said it was 'in the bailiffs hands'. Tony phoned the bailiffs who had a pre recorded message on their answer machine. I suggested hiding the furniture with the neighbours, but Mrs Dixon felt this would mean telling the neighbours her troubles which she did not want to do. She eventually decided she would have to sell her furniture to her children because they would give it back to her. Tony suggested firstly that she should ask for the bailiffs' identification; secondly that she should ask them to leave the form (suggesting that she pay £20 a week to clear the debt, an amount she could not afford), which she would then take to her solicitor's. Finally Tony advised her not to sign anything if she could not afford the repayments.

He said to me afterwards that 'there was nothing we could do' and this was 'another one for Beverley', the new social worker. Mrs Dixon had been referred to three different social workers over a number of years. If she was dealing with an urgent financial crisis she would come to see the duty social worker. Users such as Mrs Dixon were seen as having intractable financial problems and few of the social workers wanted to take them on as an on-going 'case'.

As a single parent, Mrs Dixon is likely to have lost £2.52 a week with the change from the 1987/88 supplementary benefit rates to 1988/89 income support rates. Comparing the Single Payments budget in 1985/6 with the Community Care grants budget in 1995/6, there is an 80 per cent fall in real terms (Oppenheim and Harker 1996). Mrs Dixon's experience with the Social Fund is backed up by research commissioned by the Department of Social Security and conducted by the Social Policy Research Unit at the University of York. They found that almost 70 per cent of those repaying loans said they had insufficient money to live on. Over a third said they had to cut down on food, clothing or paying bills (Huby and Dix 1992). The Children's Society, Family Service Units and Family Welfare Association (1995) have also highlighted the inadequacies of the Social Fund.

Fiscal welfare

Social service users are also less likely to benefit from tax cuts and tax reforms (Taylor Gooby and Papadakis 1985, Pond 1989) than the wealthier members of the population. Bennett and Oppenheim (1991, p.7) develop a 'welfare for the rich and welfare for the poor' example, where a married couple with a single earner on £40,000 per year would *gain* £127.45 a week in mortgage and pensions tax relief whereas an unemployed married couple with two children aged four and six would be *given* £128.61 a week in welfare benefits. Because the former couple are net contributors and the latter couple net beneficiaries, their financial benefits from the fiscal or public welfare system are not normally compared. Moreover the couple who are at present unemployed are likely to have been net contributors in the past and may be in the future. Yet they are still unlikely to gain the fiscal benefits of the middle class couple.

Social workers and the Social Fund

Social service users' increasing financial need, due to government social security policies were either not recognized by social workers because they took it for granted that social service users were poor or users' financial plight was understood but social workers felt powerless to help. These responses can be explained by examining how the social workers in Carshire and City teams dealt with the issue of the Social Fund.

Vernon (the Silverton team leader), senior welfare rights officers, and other team leaders decided to pursue a policy of non cooperation with the DSS regarding Community Care grants and Social Fund loans. This was a principled stand. It reflected unease, first, about the difficulty social security claimants would have in paying back loans thereby creating extra financial need which would result in more pressure on social services departments. Secondly, non cooperation with DSS was an assertion on the part of social workers that they were not part of the income maintenance system. Social work involvement, which could have resulted in social service users gaining priority over the grant claims of non users, might well have encouraged claimants to use social services as a second benefit agency.

However during the fieldwork at Silverton social work team when I tried to discuss the policy with individual social workers, none remembered reading the policy document. They were relieved they did not have to take on more work in relation to the DSS, and were grateful that such a decision had been taken for them by the team leader and had become departmental policy. Copies of the policy report were finally discovered in a filing cabinet by the Divisional Officer.

The local DSS office invited Silverton social workers to a meeting to discuss the Social Fund. The team leader's response to the invitation was, 'I'm not interested in the Social Fund at the moment. We have a non cooperation policy. I don't want anything to do with it'. It was agreed that Brian Lunt, the welfare rights officer, his assistant Malcolm and I would go to the meeting. The meeting also included probation officers, CAB workers and representatives from voluntary agencies for the Silverton area. Silverton DSS had only spent 35.2 per cent of their budget for grants compared to 85.43 per cent for loans for the financial year up to March. The DSS manager hoped that care organisations would encourage individuals to apply for grants by April, so that their budget was not reduced in subsequent years.

The manager explained the shortfall in the allocation of community care grants was due to: a shortage of Social Fund officers and a turnover rate of four out of five officers; minimal visiting - DSS were less of a 'care' agency and that 'home helps may see more'; and that they could not get the information from social services when they wanted to provide a grant. He concluded, 'like it or not we are stuck with it (the Social Fund) and so we have to make the best of it for the client'.

For social workers and home help organisers in the Silverton team (who knew very little about the Social Fund due to the departmental policy of non cooperation), it proved difficult to discover social service users who were eligible for community care grants within a month. However a meeting was arranged by Karen the deputy team leader after pressure from the welfare rights officer. Older people in the two neighbourhoods observed were excluded from claiming a community care grant because their savings exceeded £500. Lorna, (a home help organiser from the Silverton team) commented at the meeting, 'I can't think of one elderly person who would get the community care grant, a lot of people have savings of over £500 for their funeral, some people have up to a £1000.'

The meeting with social workers and home help organisers thus appeared unsuccessful. However, Brian, the welfare rights officer, commented that since the meeting with the local DSS he had not had any community care grant applications turned down, and had actually secured one award of £500. The policy of non cooperation with DSS carried out by the Silverton team had little effect on local or national policy though it appears to have restricted the grants paid out to claimants.

A non cooperation policy did provide some respite for Silverton social workers from dealing with users in increasingly desperate financial straits. However City team who had a policy of determined advocacy regarding the Social Fund had written to all their users prior to the implementation of the Social Security Act in 1988 stating that they would not be able to receive extra funding from social services, once single payments were withdrawn. 'Gatekeeping' actions such as this may have a similar deterrent effect for poor users to Silverton's non cooperation policy, but would allow social workers in the City team to use their discretion when applying for community care grants on behalf of particular social service users.

On the one hand some social workers, especially in the Silverton team, wished to show their disapproval of the new social security policies which had disadvantaged all claimants and gave social workers unwelcomed power in relation to social security finance and social services users. On the other hand social workers (especially in the City team) were aware that if grant monies available under the Social Fund were not utilized, the government might interpret this outcome as evidence of insufficient demand.

Social service users and the restructuring of the housing market

The rate of home ownership in Britain increased from 55 per cent in 1979 to 67 per cent in 1995, turning round the 60 year growth of council housing (Malpass 1998). However the popularity of the Conservative 'Right to Buy' policy does not tell us anything about the casualties of this policy.

The transfer of housing subsidies from the public sector to the private and voluntary sector has resulted in personal and financial difficulties for those who cannot afford the market price for housing. There is increasing evidence that people who are, for example, coming out of long stay institutions are at risk of homelessness and mental and physical ill health (Shanks and Smith 1992, Means and Smith 1994). Wherever council or social housing is available, it has acquired like social services, the stigmatised status of being available only for the poor or disadvantaged. Many people who could not really afford to buy their own property were seduced by building societies, banks and the media into taking out mortgages for which they could not meet payments.

> Some commentators stress the easy availability of credit, coupled with aggressive advertising, 'creates' a demand, and encourages people to take on commitments to a greater extent than they might if left to their own devices (Ford 1991, p.20).

Mortgages had largely been a middle class preserve. Institutions who lend money have not provided education on how the system works. They did not appear to have the time, the skills or the motivation to explain to the predominantly working class people in the areas where the fieldwork was conducted, how and in what ways the market system differed from the public housing system. Brian, the welfare rights officer for the Silverton area, commented that some building societies were particularly punitive with customers who could not afford their mortgage repayments during the 1986 miners' strike. It was assumed they would not be able to clear their debts and their houses were therefore repossessed.

> Brian: ...they couldn't clear them...the type of property that was repossessed were the little terraced ones where they had nothing to sell to get into a smaller property...individual (Building Society) managers have their quotas...the ends justifies the means.

Mr and Mrs Hallam

One family interviewed could not keep up the mortgage payments during the miners' strike and eventually posted the keys to the house through the letterbox of the Building Society. They and their six children moved to a two bed roomed housing association house. Mr Hallam gave the impression that he had not discussed his decision with personnel at the Building Society, he just became fed up with the worry of not being able to make the repayments. When he found out that a small house near to where he had grown up was empty and available from a Housing Association, he and his family moved. The living conditions in this house (in which they were interviewed) were extremely cramped, especially for the younger children. During the interview, one of the toddlers became entangled in the kettle flex, whilst another ran out of the back door into the road when Mr and Mrs Hallam were saying goodbye to me at the front. Fortunately the car approaching the toddler was able to stop. Linda, the social worker who visited them, was keen for them to move. Mr Hallam was working again, but seemed unwilling to repeat his previous experience of buying a house, even though the Housing Association had offered to let him buy the house in which he and his family were living. Mrs Hallam, according to Linda, was not so keen to stay where they were but expressed no opposition to Mr Hallam during the interview. They both talked about extending their living accommodation by converting the empty almost derelict shop next door. However Mrs Hallam had apparently said privately to Linda, 'Where would I go with six kids?'

It seems that the Thatcher government's housing and economic policies have increased individual wealth (Stark 1986, Malpass 1998) at the expense of: local authorities; those who cannot afford to buy their council house and therefore have to put up with deteriorating standards as resources for public housing dwindle; those who are forced out of the housing market into privately rented and housing association accommodation, bed and breakfast or hostels and those who have nowhere to live at all.

Eighty per cent of outstanding credit is associated with borrowing for housing and with credit hand in hand goes debt, and in some cases repossession, particularly for low income mortgagees. Janet Ford, (1991, p.32) describes this process:

> Until the late 1970s home ownership was largely the preserve of the secure professional white collar employee, and skilled crafts worker. In 1979 there were approximately 6 million mortgage loans held. In 1990 there were 9.3 million mortgage loans in force (House of Commons, Hansard 1990). This expansion is the outcome of several factors, including the increase in the number of households (particularly single person households); the impact of the right to buy legislation (with discounted prices and supportive financial arrangements); the decline in the quality and quantity of local authority rental property (with associated lengthening waiting lists); the move towards market rents; the deregulation of financial processes and increasingly competitive markets; and the clear desire of many people to own a property.

In the 1980s, the number of home owners grew as mortgage institutions increased their 'down market' lending to compensate for their problems in lending to the third world and domestic industries. Between 1982 and 1986, amongst all households headed by a manual worker, the percentage with mortgages grew from 42.9 per cent to 52.6 per cent (thus exceeding the growth among non manual households). Most were in employment *when they entered the tenure* (Office of Fair Trading 1989). However by the 1990s problems of short term working contracts, negative equity, and repossessions had become commonplace. In 1992 one in five homeowners who had bought their homes in the last five years owed more than their property was worth (Ford and Wilcox 1992). Repossessions increased from 12,400 in 1984 to 75, 540 in the peak year of 1991 and are still running at more than twice the highest ever annual rate before the 1990s (Malpass, 1998). In 1994 133,700 homeowners were between six and twelve months in arrears with their mortgage payments compared to 42,810 in 1984 (Ford 1995).

In this study social workers and users were tackling problems of low income, debt, and building societies, rather than difficulties with council housing departments. As private institutions are concerned with value for money for their shareholders, they are not likely to be as understanding as a housing department might be if people on low wages or in unstable jobs have a problem meeting their repayments. Public money is effectively being spent on social workers attempting to solve privatised financial problems. In a contracting out culture perhaps social services departments should bill these private institutions for the cost of sorting out their problems?

Mrs Bagthorpe

On the first day of the fieldwork at Silverton, I listened to a telephone request from Mrs Bagthorpe, a social service user who was in tears and asking for social work help because the Abbey National Building Society was threatening to evict her and her family (a working husband and four children) for debts of £121.85. As a postgraduate student, presumably regarded as middle class with good earning potential, I had been allowed to continue with my mortgage debt of over £900 for eighteen months without any threat of eviction. Mrs Bagthorpe had already paid £400 off her arrears and could afford £20 that day. However the building society said if the outstanding amount was not paid within forty eight hours the family would be evicted.

Karen, the social worker who had responded to the telephone call from Mrs Bagthorpe, said 'I would have to go to charities... to use Section 17 money, you would have to go to committee to get that sort of money'. She was not able to convince the building society manager that Mrs Bagthorpe would be able to pay the debt off by the following Monday from her child allowance and disability allowance (one of her children Marilyn, had severe disabilities). The building society manager said, 'This has happened a number of times in the last few years', referring to Mrs Bagthorpe getting behind with her payments. Karen then rang the Homeless Families Officer who 'twisted the arm' of the building society and arranged with them that the money 'would be paid one way or another' by the following Monday. He commented to Karen that Mrs Bagthorpe had 'got up someone's nose'. Karen then rang Mrs Bagthorpe back and said, 'You must pay the money by the following Monday otherwise it destroys social services' credibility'. Mrs Bagthorpe told Karen that she had learned her lesson. Mrs Bagthorpe's request for help had come on the same day that her daughter Marilyn (whose life expectancy was not more than five years) had had two fits at school.

I interviewed Mrs Bagthorpe later on in the fieldwork and she maintained that she had had no trouble with the mortgage repayments since, and 'it wouldn't happen again'.

> Interviewer: If you ever did get in the same situation again, would you go back to social services?
> Mrs Bagthorpe: I don't know, I don't think it would work this time with the building society. If they tried that approach again with the building society, I think they'd say 'Oh no you did it before and she didn't keep her side of the bargain'. They wouldn't be able to persuade the building society again I don't think.
> Interviewer: So it wouldn't be worth you going back to social services?
> Mrs Bagthorpe: No it would have to be a moneylender I suppose which would probably make it worse all round wouldn't it - because it's silly borrowing money to pay off arrears isn't it?
> Interviewer: I wouldn't be as definite as that about not going back to social services, because you've got your three children. (Marilyn, her daughter had died since the original crisis). It's up to you but I wouldn't be too definite about it.
> Mrs Bagthorpe: Alright flower, I won't get in that situation again (laughs).

Mrs Bagthorpe had no idea of the differing policies that were pursued as far as repayments of mortgage debts were concerned with people of different backgrounds, living in different parts of the country and being of the wrong sex or race. Although Mrs Bagthorpe was at home with her children, she seemed to be responsible for the mortgage repayments. She complained that although her husband was good company when he was in, he was out a lot and did not help with the children. Her use of the word 'I' throughout the interview when talking about the mortgage and her plan to use money she had access to (child benefit and disability allowance) implied that she held herself responsible for the debt. This was her second mortgage (she had been responsible for the mortgage and two other children in a previous marriage). She had none of her own kin family living locally to help her financially or in other ways.

Parker (1987) has argued that the roots of debt may lie in the pattern of financial allocation adopted, and the inadequate allocation to women for day to day budgeting may push them to miss payments due. A number of studies have indicated that the internal allocation of resources is informed by a cultural acceptance by both men and women that a portion of the household's money is 'protected' as 'the man's money' (Morris 1984). Parker has shown how even when debts are incurred the 'man's money' remains protected. Ford's

(1990) study of owner occupiers in default reported that the majority of households effected some reorganisation and reallocation of finances when the mortgage crisis became sufficiently serious. The reallocations were not equitable but the inequalities were reduced.

> Even where commitments have been the man's responsibility, women may manage them when they become debts because of their role as day to day financial managers. Here the assumption is that it is they who can re-jig the budgets and make economies, an assumption women often confirm, but only by personally bearing the brunt of any economies...debt involves negotiating with creditors, visiting their offices, undertaking to make certain payments. Women are also often seen as 'free' to undertake this work, either because their own employment is part time, or regarded as less significant than the man's, or because they are 'at home' all day involved with tasks that are accorded little priority or prestige (Ford 1991, p.81).

Brady's (1987) in depth study of seven families in debt reported that women had a higher incidence of self assessed mental health problems than men. Stress factors he associated with debt included: the stigma of debt; financial adversity; attempts to cope financially; the guilt and blame associated with failure and the isolation of women. Lone mothers according to the PSI survey of credit and debt, had 'exceptional' level of risk. 'More than four out of ten lone parents had one or more problem debts; almost one in seven were in serious debt, owing money on three or more commitments' (Berthoud and Kempson 1990). Debt was a common difficulty for the social service users observed and interviewed during the fieldwork.

Mrs Crale

Mrs Crale came to social services as a one parent family with two children dependent on income support. Her husband was claiming tax relief for the mortgaged house that she and the children were living in. He was working in Saudi Arabia and was having an affair with a nurse. This had eventually split up the marriage, and while the husband and his mistress were apparently having expensive holidays, his wife was claiming income support and food vouchers from social services because she did not have enough to live on. Mrs Crale still seemed to be hoping that her husband would come back to her, so no adequate financial provision had been made for her or the children.

> Mrs Crale: I came (to social services) to see if anyone could help me 'cos my house was actually up for sale at the time and I was going to

be homeless...nothing really happened (as a result of the first visit to social services) because my husband decided he was quite happy for the house not to be sold - 'it's not fair' he said, 'because of the boys'.
Interviewer: So what happened the second time you came in?
Mrs Crale: I came down because I had no money for food and owed £26 for the gas bill and I owed £11, two weeks electric that was, ...so it left me with virtually nothing to live on...I know I bought ten cigarettes but I have to... But I was just really upset because I'd nothing for the children and I can't stand to see kids go hungry. (Mr Crale was not helping with the bills but had agreed to a voluntary payment of £20 per week for the children which was taken off Mrs Crale's £74 a week income support)...It's a lot of money I know (the £80 a month maintenance), but when you've got bills to pay and clothes for the children and when it's school I've got to give them money for dinners and get them tea, and because its the holidays they want to go to the swimming baths and cinema...it's a hell of a struggle, it's terrible...I just wish he'd come back....We had no problems with money when we were married.... He was great, he was fabulous, he helped me in every way possible, he's given me a lovely home and we always had food in ...brilliant with the kids...he's just a womanizer. It's only since he left I got myself into a mess with money...because with his job I was getting £350 a week for a wage. He paid all his wages home into a bank account...he said to me 'that's for the mortgage and everything else'...it was great you can understand it.
Interviewer: So you dropped from £350 a week to £74 a week apart from the mortgage. That's a big drop!
Mrs Crale: It's terrible I've always been used to having that money.

Mrs Crale had received advice from social services regarding council housing and on her second visit a £10 food voucher to feed the children. Mrs Crale unlike Mrs Bagthorpe had financial problems because of a sudden drop in income rather than persistent low income. Her house and its furnishings and her clothes were of a higher standard than most social service users I visited. However she and her sons may have to get used to different accommodation and a lower standard of living.

Sullivan (1986) and Tunnard (1973) indicate that divorced and separated women face considerable housing difficulties. They may initially remain in the matrimonial home, but the costs prove prohibitive and debts result. They may experience 'forced' moves out of single owner occupancy into public renting, sharing or even homelessness. As Ford (1991 p.60) notes,

...where the lone parent who remains in the matrimonial home following the dissolution of a relationship is a woman, the available income is, in many cases, low and there is a high risk of mortgage default.

More lucrative employment opportunities, better child care facilities, and fairer maintenance and access arrangements could change this scenario in the future. However the restructuring of the housing market has meant that women with children who cannot afford to maintain a mortgage are marginalised like all the other non owner occupiers, in some cases having to rely on bed and breakfast accommodation.

It was fairly unusual, in the City team, for social services to be asked for help with mortgage problems. They were seen as middle class problems not the problems of the poor. For example, Keith in the City team could get no free legal help for June's mortgage problem because the Law Centres would not deal with the buying of council houses, 'they were against it in principle'. However as Ford (1991, p.27) comments, '...in many cases they (mortgagees) do have household earnings that are below the low pay threshold as defined by the Low Pay Unit or the Council of Europe.'

June

June had been discharged from Rampton mental hospital on appeal. She had been there since she was 13 and she was now 22. Loan sharks had told her she could buy her City council flat at £5 a week, the total cost being £1000 and the deposit being £25. She would not agree to sign anything until she had talked to Keith, her social worker. He was taking her to a solicitors for half an hour's legal advice for £5 as she had already paid the deposit. The solicitor advised her to withdraw from the scheme and ask for the return of her deposit. We are all dependent on government organisations, only some of them are labelled welfare organisations (Titmuss 1956). It is these organisations that the government expects us to secure our independence from. In June's case it seems clear that becoming independent from her social worker, and dependent on a private financial organisation in order to secure her 'emancipation' from institutional care and from council housing would have resulted in exploitation. She would also of course have benefited from tax relief if the arrangement had been genuine. All individuals gain from the state in different ways depending on their income, despite the differing terminologies that are used to describe our indebtedness to the state. Benefits are regarded as an example of government generosity whilst tax relief on mortgages and pensions are seen as relieving the burden of government taxation (Cook 1989). Those on benefit are understood to be beneficiaries of government largesse while they are claiming, which may be preceded by years of being tax contributors, nevertheless claimants tend to be labelled as 'scroungers'. Tax relief on mortgages did not commence in

1979 but as Johnson (1990, p.156) comments:

> The ideology of the three Thatcher governments is more clearly demonstrated in housing than in any other area of social policy...Between 1978/79 and 1989/90 government expenditure on housing in real terms declined by 79 per cent.

Tax relief to the individual home owner and housing benefit to the individual claimant have taken the resources that were previously allocated for the whole community. This individualistic concept of redistribution does not account for those who cannot get onto the first rung of the owner-occupier ladder or who get onto it and then slip off, because of redundancy, low wages, loss of pay or marital breakdown.

Many of the social service users with financial and housing problems were female lone parents with young or school age children. As it is mostly women who take the main caring role when marriages split up, it is they who are most likely to suffer from the effects of social security and housing restructuring. Social services are involved in the privatisation of the housing market in that they are dealing with some of the casualties of it (Fabricant and Burghardt 1992). There has been an increase in money advice centres, but there is a current imbalance between the limited supply, and the great demand. Moreover the stability of such centres is extremely fragile given the current squeeze on local authority resources. It has been suggested that creditors have some responsibility to support the casualties of the credit system. Social workers may prefer to see creditors supporting money advice centres rather than social work departments, thereby reducing the extra financial services expected of social workers.

> Compulsory mechanisms to fund money advice - for example, a levy on creditors - are discussed from time to time and may yet be necessary...The underlying problems that give rise to much of the debt, particularly in low income households, have been influenced and structured not only by the policies of some creditors, but centrally by the economic and welfare policies pursued by successive governments in the 1980's (Ford 1991, p.103).

Social Housing

Social work is clearly not just dealing with the casualties of mortgage repossessions, but also with the immense shortage of social housing. Social service users with marital and/or poverty problems, or who are moving out of residential institutions, cannot be rehoused satisfactorily when in need. In terms of the shortage of suitable housing for users in crisis situations, the dilemma for social workers centred around how to prioritise their time and use the resources available effectively. For example in one observed crisis case, it took three city social workers working together very effectively, more than three days to rehouse a lone parent with four children. Since 1981 the total council housing stock in City had dropped from 94,000 to 56,000 and over the same period, the waiting list has increased from 35,000 to 56,000.

By the mid 1990s local authorities' building programmes had ground to a halt. Capital expenditure was devoted either to renovation of the existing stock or loans to Housing Associations to build new dwellings. Although Housing Associations enjoyed a major expansion of their capital programmes supported by government grants, they have only recently started to employ social workers and home care workers to support people with learning disabilities, mental illness and those who are they are rehousing in the community. Local authority and government contracts *did not* specify this type of support. Meanwhile since the peak year of 1992/3 there have been cuts in grants from the Housing Corporation each year. In 1997/8, the cut was 75 per cent of the 1992/3 level (Malpass 1998). However the Labour Government has released almost £1billion from the sale of council houses for local authorities to improve social housing and £3.6 billion for repairs. A new £145 million cross government strategy to tackle the problem of rough sleeping has also been agreed. These and a number of other measures to improve social housing will need to be evaluated.

Conclusions

This chapter has suggested that the restructuring of the social security system and the housing market has created additional pressures for social service users and social workers. Many of the users' predicaments described have not been created by social workers' individual attitudes and actions, but by conservative government policies developed over the last eighteen years. The aim of this chapter has been to show how wider forces create pressures for social service users and social workers. As neither group were able to alter national policy agendas significantly, there was a sense of frustration and anger in relation to social security and housing issues which some social workers were able to escape by moving into different areas of work or out of the social work profession altogether. Social service users and carers did not have the same choice.

The day to day practice issues that arose in the fieldwork as a result of welfare restructuring can be summarised in terms of the issues of social workers providing income maintenance and crisis care. Social workers were confronted on a daily basis with social service users who needed financial aid. Such users were:

- no longer able to claim special needs payments,
- had arranged loans from the Social Fund which were causing them additional problems,
- lone parents with low cost housing needs, which could not be easily fulfilled by the private housing market.

Crisis situations which occurred were often concerned with female lone parents who needed to escape a violent partner, but where suitable housing was not available in the private, public or voluntary sector.

The Labour Government has promised the phased release of capital receipts from the sale of council houses, the removal of compulsory competitive tendering for local authorities' housing management and the repeal of restrictions on the rights of homeless people introduced in the Housing Act of 1996. However they are constrained by their pledge to keep within the Conservative Government's spending plans for the first two years of parliament and the higher priority given to health and education. Malpass (1998 p. 186) notes,

> ...Housing strategies built around privatisation and marketisation have had their day. It is now clear that what is needed is a new commitment to policies that will resolve the tensions inherent in the relationship between housing, social security and the labour market by recognising the benefits of intervention and the necessity of increased public expenditure if the serious problems of quality, quantity and affordability are to be tackled effectively.

Income support

In relation to changes in income support, visits to social services by users who had not sufficient finances to get through the week, sometimes because of Social Fund repayments, were often perceived as 'crises' by users but were not necessarily defined in the same way by social workers. The dilemma these issues caused for social work staff centred around their wish to be seen as a caring profession and yet being unable to satisfy users' needs when they came to social services for help. Social workers attempted to resolved their dilemma in relation to income maintenance by developing policies to show their antipathy to the social security changes they were faced with, thus hoping to alleviate their low morale and protest to the government about the extra work that such policies were creating for them. In practice many of the social workers observed found it difficult to refuse financial help to users and the dilemmas this caused them in terms of attitudes and actions are discussed in more detail in chapter 6. There was little evidence in the fieldwork that the social work policies of non cooperation and determined advocacy were effective in disrupting social security offices and government departments. Unfortunately social service users and other claimants appeared caught in the conflict between the DSS and SSDs and were sometimes confused or misled or were not able to claim their entitlements. It is worth emphasising the point made earlier in the chapter, that although for some social workers the policies on the Social Fund enabled them to make a principled stand, for others it was a way of ignoring poverty issues. As Hill (1990, p.133) notes:

> The official non-cooperation stance does offer a way to deal with the new situation, but it also provides an encouragement to the view that social workers must treat the material circumstances of their clients as something they can do nothing about. While some would call that getting back to 'real social work', others would view it as the ultimate encouragement to 'cop out' and disregard poverty's causal role in other social problems.

At the present time, the Labour Government's plans to revamp social security are concerned with improving access to the formal labour market which may help some social service users such as lone parents, young people and those in the field observations who were unemployed. However a more far reaching and radical reform of social security would be the citizens' basic income model which is receiving increasing support from a wide variety of intellectual and political arenas throughout Europe and is discussed in more detail in Chapter 8 (McKay, 1998).

3 Methodological perspectives

The chapter begins by analysing theoretical concepts and their relationship to the methods used in the research, and proceeds to consider issues such as: employing group discussions and interviews; conducting a participant observation study; action research; and the policy implications of the study for the two teams involved. Finally, the research methods are evaluated in terms of what developed as the best integration of theory and method to evaluate social work practice.

Relating theory and method

Figures 3.1 and 3.2 provide a philosophical foundation from which to explain the perspectives employed, and suggest that although different methods can be used to examine one perspective, to describe a method in isolation from its theoretical root is sterile and promotes a 'cookbook' approach to methodology (Smith 1988). Having described and analysed the research in terms of interests (Figure 3.1), and methodological concerns (Figure 3.2), the chapter presents a critique of these ways of understanding the relationship between method and theory. By using examples from the fieldwork, it is suggested that the boundaries dividing the various interests and methodological concerns are too rigid when compared to the reality of the research setting.

A critique

Research is too often dominated by a theoretical structure which fails to take

	Ontological Concerns		
	Practical	Technical	Emancipatory
	Humanistic philosophies (excluding idealism). Realities contingent on human encounter. Reality present in appearance.	Objective positivism. Reality is independent of observers and actors. Reality present in appearance.	Structuralism, reality hidden. Objective positivism. Reality is independent of observers and actors.
Method			
	Subjective meanings investigated and interactions with others in important roles. Crucial link between attitudes to poverty and actions. Field observation.	1. Evidence on percentage of claimants who are clients. 2. Survey results on social workers' attitudes to poverty (Becker 1987). 3. Survey results on social work students. 4. Social survey results on responses to social work and poverty.	Results of empirical research highlighted for structural change.
Epistemological Concerns			
	Empirical Research ↑↓ Interactive Theory (integrative) Social Workers' trajectories through time and space - attitudes and actions in relation to poverty.	Empirical Research ↓ Evidence led theory Theory Theories on social workers', students' and users' attitudes to poverty and social work.	Theory ↓ Theory led research Empirical Research Social Workers' attitudes and actions in relation to poverty reinforce conflict theory

Figure 3.1 Method and theory integration - Methodological concerns

Practical	Technical	Emancipatory
Disclose world of common sense meaning How social workers, students and users come to 'know' in training and in work.	Prediction Control What do social workers, tutors, students, users, CCETSW, social work managers, think about the relationship between poverty and social work.	Self Reflective, move to more rational society Examine power structure in which social workers, students and users operate.
Communication - interaction Can awareness of poverty (like awareness of sexism and racism) be taught? How?	Labour - How systems work Where social workers/students/users are located within systems. Cost/Benefit analysis.	Domination/Liberation Change in power structure necessary for social service users to reveal their true interests.
Historical Hermeneutic Science Objective body of social work knowledge - built up over time. Meanings attached to knowledge.	Empirical, Analytic Science, Quantitative Analysis Secondary and primary source material on 1) Claimants who are social work clients 2) Attitudes to social work and poverty.	Critical Theory The influence of the State, its laws, ideologies, social control. Social workers, users and the welfare state. The restructuring of welfare.
Interpretive What is meant by awareness of poverty? Does this knowledge/awareness change when roles from student to worker change?	Causal Why do users, social work tutors, CCETSW social service managers, students and social workers have particular attitudes and beliefs on the relationship between poverty and social work?	Explanatory Understanding Explaining the relationship between social work and poverty within a structural base?

Figure 3.2 Method and theory integration - Interests

account of those aspects of practice which conflict with the structure. Practice is not allowed to influence theory and this can mean that the practice itself remains undeveloped. An integrative approach is therefore adopted, which uses the Figures as a methodological foundation, but does not limit interests and ontological and epistemological concerns into separate compartments.

The impossibility of defining rigid boundaries within and between the categories described on the tables became evident during the field observation of social workers. For example, I came to the conclusion that social workers' attitudes and actions in relation to poverty are partly determined by the meanings they continue to develop as individuals in interaction with others, and partly are a result of the structures and institutions that surround them. Thus the mode of analysis for the research has both emancipatory and practical interests (see Figure 3.1).

Emancipatory interests and concerns

The idea of emancipatory interests is of itself problematic. In interviewing users of the social services, the methodological aim was to give them some recorded, independent time and space to put their view of the service offered them. In practice the role of a researcher may not be considered by social service users to be particularly liberating. Would they want to reveal their concerns in a way that they might to a family member or friend when my interactions with them were mediated by social services? The issue of social control is one that does not just apply to social workers' relationships with social service users, but also to researchers (Bell and Encell 1976).

The idea of feminist research is that it is emancipatory - it tries to understand the mechanisms of oppression and its objective is 'opening channels for change'. This is not to imply that only feminist research is emancipatory, nor that it is necessarily only emancipatory of and for women (Morgan 1981). Bringing women's values, interests and social position into the limelight through methodologies that value gender differences questions the traditional approach to social research which ignores gender as a crucial variable (Goldthorpe 1984). Although the research perspective is feminist, how does this operate in a study of social work and poverty? Emancipation can be defined as 'setting free from some form of restraint', but enabling one group of individuals to have their say can hinder other groups from feeling free to express themselves. By giving a voice to for example male working class users in the research, female middle class social workers may feel oppressed and criticised from below as well as from the male social work hierarchy above them. Some of the social workers in the fieldwork talked about how they felt unsupported at home, because their male partners were not interested in and did not want to talk about social work. One unqualified social worker told me she was a 'different person' at home. 'Emancipatory interests' cover a number of different issues which cannot necessarily be reconciled.

Technical interests and concerns

Technical interests and concerns also did not appear as straightforward in practice as the initial theoretical diagrams suggested. Gathering primary data from referral books on the number of financial inquiries from people coming to social services, was in this case, mediated by practical and hermeneutic concerns. For example after four out of nine months of field observation with the Silverton social work team, the receptionist told me that if she received a straightforward financial query from a social service user, she sent them to the welfare rights adviser in the Enterprise Centre without recording them in the referral book. All referrals were supposed to be reported and such a practice would significantly affect the numbers of individuals recorded by social services as having financial problems. It is also worth investigating the meaning behind such an action. Does the ideology of the social work team give the impression to the receptionist that they are not interested in social service users who have financial problems? Or is she aware that users prefer the service they get from the welfare rights advisers?

The problem of defining and quantifying technical data in relation to this research was also apparent during the field observations when some visits and interviews with social service users were not written up as being concerned with financial problems, when to the researcher (also a qualified social worker) they appeared to be intimately connected with material deprivation.

The Silverton area in which the social work team was based had more referrals of all kinds than other areas in the authority. The divisional officer thought this was because the social workers were based in the Town Hall next to the housing department and so people could deal with two departments at once. In the Carley area where individual users were apparently equally poor, they found it difficult in terms of time and finances to travel to the social work offices because they were more isolated.

That reality is not present in the superficial presentation of statistics is confirmed by observations of one of the social services welfare rights offices. One of the welfare rights officers admitted that she sometimes made up welfare rights referral figures because 'I know what people want'. She appeared to be referring to her immediate boss and social services management rather than users.

So it seems that statistics on poverty related referrals to social workers or welfare rights workers may not be reliable. Their occurrence and meaning depends on the individuals who direct, record and analyse referrals. There are also a number of reasons why users may go to one social work office but not another. These examples illustrate the blurring of boundaries between methods and theory and differing ontological and epistemological concerns.

Boundaries

Boundaries can also be blurred because one method leads on to another. It was only by following my interest in the technical aspects of the research - what social workers think about poverty, using primary and secondary quantitative data, that I realized that actions may contradict attitudes. Thus I became more interested in the interpretative domain of inquiry and qualitative data (see Figure 3.2).

Technical, practical and emancipatory interests are often interdependent and rightly so, because it is only by considering them in this way that a three dimensional model of the relationship between social work and poverty can be achieved. As Lakatos (1978, p.179) suggests: 'one research programme supersedes another if it has excess truth content over its rival, in the sense that it predicts progressively all that its rival truly predicts and more besides.'

So although Becker (1987) completed a large quantitative survey and in depth interviews with social workers on their attitudes to poverty, this ethnographic work follows his conclusions through, with the added dimension of a discussion on how attitudes are related to actions. P.K. Edwards (1983, p.7) suggests that 'progressive problem shifts' are in fact aiming towards truth as a goal '...even though absolute truth is impossible.' This however assumes moving from one idea and method to another is cumulatively 'progressive'.

The approach applied to this study could be described as a continuum where differing theoretical perspectives complement the methods used. Both emancipatory and realist perspectives and all methodologies have been important and I would not want to see the world only from one perspective, as Harvey (1988) suggests, if this means defining out particular theoretical concerns or methodologies.

The Figures then, are a general analysis of the main theoretical and practical areas that this study has covered. They are not intended to suggest rigid boundaries between the theoretical areas of interest and the methodologies that have been used to investigate them. My aim is to highlight the connections rather than the divisions between emancipatory, technical and practical perspectives and quantitative and qualitative research, in order to give a fuller picture of what is occurring in the relationships between social workers, social service users and social work students.

A discussion on the nature of subjectivity

A subjective approach to research methodology implies that social enquiry takes place in a particular context, that it is a social and political activity, not just a set of techniques to be applied to the world 'out there' (Burgess 1988). The number of descriptions, rules, methods, and theories militates against there being one right objective way to collect quantitative information, conduct group discussion and in depth interviews, and be a participant, sometimes a non participant observer.

Triangulation

Denzin's classic concept of triangulation is worth considering in relation to this research. He argues that 'sociology's empirical reality is a reality of competing definitions, attitudes and personal values' (Denzin 1970, p.300), and therefore multiple methods and theoretical approaches must be used. He proposes four basic triangulations:

1. Data with respect to time, place, person and level. Group discussions with students and social workers and observations of various types of social work meetings have provided rich data where the topic is the same but the time and place have varied, or where individuals of different rankings or occupations are observed in the same time and place, for example case conference meetings.

2. Between multiple observers of the same phenomenon. Social workers' and users' views of the same situation have been compared, as have students' views of their social work courses and social workers' of a team issue.

3. Between multiple theoretical perspectives with respect to the same set of objects (see Figures).

4. Methodological triangulation which involves between method triangulation using dissimilar methods to measure the same unit; and within method triangulation which would employ variations within the same basic methodology. Between method triangulation has been achieved by conducting a survey with social work students and interviewing them singly and in group discussion. Field observation of social workers included an understanding of policy documents and a quantitative study of referral rates. Variations within the same basic methodology have included: field observations which analyse social workers' attitudes and actions were compared with the results from interviewing users and observing users in

the social services waiting room; interviewing social workers individually was compared with their comments and participation in feedback group discussions on social work and poverty. However in some cases the results have been different and cannot be integrated. For example social workers' attitudes in group discussion or interviews have not been congruent with their actions during field observation.

Even when the same method is used throughout a research project, the data can be interpreted in different ways. If a variety of methods are used, the problems could be compounded. However Robert Walker (1985, p.16) notes,

> ...research findings are constantly being evaluated and interpreted by the writers, readers and users of research in the light of their information needs. ...An understanding of the methodological heritage of a particular technique is a necessary element in the interpretive process but in the end each person makes his (sic) own evaluation.

Qualitative methods

Walker suggests choosing to use qualitative methods '...may reflect limitations in the state of the quantitative art or a philosophical stance that quantification is inappropriate'(p.21). For example the City social work team operated on a community work 'patch' model. They knew many of the people asking for help and therefore did not write each request on a referral sheet. It was therefore difficult to quantify objectively how many requests for financial help they had received. Unfortunately a later Audit Commission report on City Social Services was not able to review their social work practice in the ethnographic style utilised in this book.

Throughout my field experiences, I was struck by the fact that social existence is disordered, ambiguous and humanly messy (and this applies to the researchers as well as to the researched); yet we try to make sense of the social world with methods that are conspicuously unable to take account of this messiness, and which appear stainless, sanitised and inappropriate in comparison to the subject matter. The conventions of scientific exposition where the steps involved in proving or disproving a hypothesis are presented in logical order protects the researcher from queries about her motives, methods and assumptions and confirms professional detachment and rigour. Take for example time. It is a crucial variable and cannot be held constant, thus violating one of the basic precepts underlying the hypothetico/deductive method. How do I know that a person participating in group discussion at Time A is the same person at a later Time B? How do I know that I as the researcher have responded in the same way to an individual I interviewed at

Time A as at Time B?

One cannot ignore or under emphasize the social and political context of research, nor pretend that social researchers are disinterested value - neutral automatons. The failure of the sociological imagination as C. Wright Mills demonstrated, is to **not** understand that personal research accounts can construct a bridge between private issues and public concerns.

> Above all, seek to develop and to use the sociological imagination. Avoid the fetishism of method and technique...Know that the human meaning of public issues must be revealed by relating them to personal troubles - and to the problems of the individual life. Know that the problems of social science when adequately formulated, must include both troubles and issues, both biography and history, and the range of their intricate relations (Mills 1970, p.248).

A feminist methodology

This research is not on women alone or for and with women only. However, as a female researcher I have been aware that my view of the world in relation to the interactions I have observed and noted are likely to be different to that of a man doing the same research. Most social work students, social workers and users I have worked with have been female, while social work academics, team leaders, and social work management have been generally male. The subject of the research - social work - is traditionally a 'caring' area which is seen as part of women's role (Finch and Groves 1983, Williams 1989, Dominelli 1991). Social work can be defined as women's work within a hierarchical, patriarchal management and training structure (Hudson 1989).

It is the nature of the subject of the investigation, and how that investigation is carried out, that determines whether research can be said to be concerned with feminist issues. The paradigm shift that feminism contributes to methodology is not classifying qualitative research as particularly female but creating the thinking whereby all good research has to take into account women's views and actions as having equal importance with those of men's, with a theoretical questioning of any differences in male and female perspectives (Roberts 1990).

Sue Kingsley (1985) suggests that a feminist method would be one which validates the perceptions of the people at the focus of the study - that is one which challenges the barriers between researcher and researched and takes explicit account of subjectivity. She suggests that action research, embodying concepts of change, dialogue and a two way relationship between theory and practice, could offer a way out of the methodological impasse in which feminist researchers feel trapped - how is research *for* women as well as by them and on them?

Inter-subjectivity

Developing methods which make use of interpersonal understanding and empathy ('inter-subjectivity') rather than subject - object relations was not so easy in practice. Karen, one of the social workers I had come to know well, began to ask me to go to aerobics classes and tea at her house afterwards. I had to decline because other members of the team with whom she was not so popular, would have been less likely to feel they could talk to me if I was identified as her friend. The reasons I gave to her, were that as a researcher I had to treat all members of the team similarly. The discussions between myself and many of the women in both teams tended to be more personal than the discussions I had with the males. These discussions could be defined as 'women's talk' in that they were about their life experiences, relationships and children. The conversations with the male members of the team were more likely to be about politics, films, television or sport. 'Women's talk' was an effective, mutually supportive way of gaining rapport and went some way to achieving Kingsley's ideal of 'inter-subjective' methods.

Women's talk

Johnson (1975, p.136-7), despite conducting a participant observation study of American social work teams with high numbers of female staff, concludes:

> In an interview conducted during the final week of the observations at Metro, I asked one female CWS worker if she thought my sex made a difference in her actions throughout the research. I asked if she thought she might have done anything differently if I had been a woman. ...She advanced the supposition that she engaged in more 'woman-talk' when in the company of other women. She observed she had done less of this on the days we had been together...In retrospect I've developed a sense that the ambiguous differences hinted at by this social worker are indeed real ones. With an admittedly limited understanding of 'woman-talk' however, my conclusion is that the kind of information one gets from engaging in it is not directly related to the knowledge I sought during the research.

Participating in 'women's talk' is important in this research in the way participating in 'men's talk' might be essential in conducting a participant observation study of the police force - it achieves rapport (Holdaway 1982). For example Mary in the Silverton team who for her own reasons had as little contact with me as possible. She had been off work because her father had died and while offering my condolences, we became involved in a discussion about family relationships which we both found useful and supportive. Not long after this discussion when I was still in her office, she confided in me for the first time about a young girl, an incest survivor she was working with, whose (male) therapist had said 'the family wants you out of its hair'. The father was in prison and the mother and children were dependent on income support so the social worker was questioning the practicality of a teenage girl making her own way to see the therapist, in a large city 50 miles away without Mary's financial and emotional support. Up until this point, Mary had had little time for discussing the research issues. As she only worked part time, Mary took the girl in her own time and in her own car to see the therapist.

Group discussion

De Almeida (1980, p.117) suggests that participants in a group discussion cannot be considered as individuals in a sample:

> One can visualize an ideal universe of cognitive behaviour (or values, attitudes, motivations) and say that each group discussion is one single observation of such a universe.

People can also feel nervous about uttering views opposed to the rest of the group or will feel inhibited about expressing views about their department or social work course or placements in front of the researcher and/or other members of the group (Hedges 1985). Robson (1988) proposes that people tend to be more open and creative in groups because they are *more* likely to confide their personal views and opinions when they are part of a group with whom they feel familiar and relaxed. Whether or not individuals or a group feel relaxed may depend on the extent of the actual or perceived power relationship between interviewer and interviewees.

Power in groups

Social service users, who as a group were less powerful than social work students or social workers, appeared more confident and open when interviewed with family and/or friends present, than those who were interviewed alone. Approximately a third of the interviews with social service users took place when friends, relatives or both partners were present, and in these circumstances users were more likely to express negative feelings towards social workers and sometimes towards the researcher. There were situations where empathy did develop between the researcher and the usually female respondent and 'women's talk' as discussed earlier in this chapter, was often an important factor.

Social workers where the power balance was towards the professionals rather than the sole researcher tended to present views that were far more uniform in the group than when interviewed or observed individually.

Social work students demonstrated a wider range of views in the group discussions than the social workers and were not intimidated by the researcher as social service users tended to be. They had spent over a year training together and were used to expressing their views articulately in an academic environment.

Power relationships within the social worker and social work student groups were also evident in that women in the groups tended to defer to men, although black male students did not appear less assertive than white male students in expressing their opinions. In the social service user groups, males tended to defer to female respondents because women appeared to take the lead in dealing with personal, domestic and financial issues within the family and in dealing with social services (Davis and Brook 1985).

Other factors which affected what was revealed in the group discussions included: the personalities of the group and the moderator; various external factors such as the time and place when a particular issue is discussed; and what is going on for everybody in their own lives.

The benefits of group discussion

Group discussion as a research method is regarded as useful by many commentators because: it explores the force with which people express their opinions in relation to others; gives a broad range of comparative and contrasting experiences; is creative and stimulating in that people bounce ideas off each other, come up with new ones and sometimes change their attitudes and behaviour. It also provides actors with a unique opportunity to negotiate their competing definitions of reality and to learn from their experience with the research process. Theoretical models for group discussion include: the 'forming, storming, norming, performing and mourning' model; group feedback analysis; action research; transactional analysis; group 'language'; and the psychodynamics of groups. In practical terms, there are conflicting 'agreed rules' on organizing and conducting group discussions on issues such as: recruiting, the size of groups, reconvened groups, pre existing groups, focussed groups, delphi groups, projective techniques, the moderator, incentives and the time needed for group discussion.

Participant observation - a reflexive account

The researcher was aware that her subjective view of the social world resulted in the selection of particular events for discussion. This does not necessarily mean the themes and connections proposed are invalid. It merely alerts the reader to possible selective attention to events that were thought significant in the research. Nor is this the same as a confession that the researcher's personal or political agenda has dominated the research. There is however no complete answer as to how the reader integrates the researcher's perspective into the research findings, apart from having a thorough understanding of what perspectives are being used.

Field observation of a social services team has been an important method used in the research, because it explores a new way of understanding the relationship between social workers' attitudes and actions in relation to poverty. However this method is particularly prone to questions about how the researcher's interactions with the field affected the nature of the findings.

Participant and non participant observation are difficult to define as different and separate - the social workers' responses to having a researcher in their midst as well as my responses to them have sometimes meant participating in the work of the team and sometimes taking a more detached role. The fact that the Silverton team leader offered me a job with the team, and the team organised a special meal and leaving present on my last day, suggests that the process of the researcher becoming integrated into the team was successful. However it is an emotionally difficult balancing act, where one wants to become close enough to the team to discover useful information but not too close so they feel betrayed. As part of the integrative process, boundaries between participating and not participating in the team's work also become blurred. As a qualified social worker when did my views for example become part of the participant rather than non participant process?

Covert and overt observation

There is a similar debate about the artificiality of a rigid distinction between covert and overt observation. I was more overt than some advisers thought I should be in explaining the aims of the research, giving feedback at the end of the observation period, and sending papers on the research before the final writing up stage. I believed it was important that social workers knew what I was doing beforehand and had an opportunity to debate the findings afterwards. However when one of the team asked me what exactly I was writing in my field notebook, I could not give her a totally straight answer. I wrote down what I thought the team were doing and saying at the time. Do I want to be overt about that? As an observer, what I said and did changed from overt to covert on a day to day almost minute to minute basis. Reflexivity is defined as the subjective nature of research being integrated into the whole, and is one aspect of methodology that has been credited to women's view of the world (Barry 1989).

My interest in ethnographic research has been a gradual stepping down process, a curiosity as to whether the tales written on questionnaires by the one hundred and fifty social work students I surveyed, and discussed on tapes by students in group discussions, were really going on in social services teams. I was also aware from personal experience, that surveys and interviews on social workers' attitudes to poverty (Becker 1987) were not necessarily the same as the reality 'on the job'.

Being a detached youth worker working mainly with girls in Liverpool and supervised by Howard Parker, gave me insights into how to observe/work in an extremely loose structure as he had done (see View from the Boys, 1974) and the determination to write it up this time. Being a qualified and experienced social worker gave me the confidence to feel I could become a socialised stranger in a social work team. It has meant easier access, difficult as it was at first, to senior management and a common professional language with all of the social work teams visited. For example what does 'Well I've done locum, so I know how to fit in quickly as far as duty's concerned' mean to the outsider? I could compare working tales with social workers in the Silverton and City teams, thus gaining their trust to the extent that I was often asked for advice or support.

Access

> For the researcher, access is controlled by the locally powerful and can determine the nature of the research findings. '...to get into the whale in the first place may need their permission and sponsorship...' (Bell and Encel 1976, p.33).

Research with social work students, social service users and to some extent social workers, confirms the idea that most social research is done on the relatively powerless for the relatively powerful. 'Studying up' rather than 'studying down' is more useful in understanding how systems and structures create events and knowledge for the powerless. The field observation in two social work teams was the 'studying up' development in this study. However, only one of the two team leaders was willing to be observed at work, and none of the social services hierarchy above those in social work teams was involved to any great extent.

We have, for example, used deception, unobtrusive measures, and power relationships to obtain data for many years. The difference is that we have used these measures, with the knowledge and approval of higher elites, against the less powerful participants in organisations. With the complicity of higher elites, we have become participant observers in mental hospitals or work groups, stood behind one way mirrors...I am suggesting not so much new techniques, but the application of existing ones at the elite level of bureaucratic structures (Spencer 1982, p.134).

In researching social work teams, there were not quite as many problems as Gary Spencer's in gaining access to West Point Military Academy. However there were Kafkaesque moments. For example one social services research officer was very dubious about giving me the work telephone number of a teamleader whose team had expressed an interest in my research and wanted to meet me. He seemed to want everything to be arranged through him, so three telephone calls became necessary not one. There were few problems obtaining access to social service users or social work students which implies that social workers have professional and bureaucratic power that other groups do not have.

The role of a participant observer

To illustrate the settling in process, I will describe how members of the Silverton team offered their help with the research.

Tony

Tony, one of the part time social workers based in the same room, was willing to take me to different sorts of cases, but apologised that this first one was not really to do with poverty and I might find it quite boring. Mr Farmer was on his own with five children in an area where the small council houses were boarded up across the road, and there were no cars apart from one Reliant Robin. Mr Farmer's house was poorly decorated and cramped. We could just about squeeze in the kitchen to talk to him, although only two out of the three of us could sit down as there was not room for more than two chairs. His eldest stepson Neil had been stealing money from him so the father, who was on income support, did not have enough for the other children. Neil also used to run away and the father could not afford the fares to keep getting him back. Neil was admitted to residential care but continued to run away. Social workers had to go and pick him up. Tony was under pressure to find somewhere else for Neil as social services officers were saying they could not afford to keep him in care after he was sixteen. The interview between Tony and Mr Farmer was interesting in that Mr Farmer was concerned about his financial situation and moving from the council house the family were living in, but not being able to because he was in arrears with the rent, while Tony was concerned about Neil and what was going to happen to him when he reached sixteen. Financial difficulties were the main agenda item for both social service user and social worker, but in Tony's case the agenda was covert. Consequently the interaction seemed to have crossed purposes with neither individual responding to what the other was saying. Discussing the situation afterwards Tony agreed that if the father was in different financial circumstances Neil may not have behaved in the same way and his father may not have asked the social services to help. If Social Services were not in financial difficulties, Tony would not have been faced with the difficulty of where Neil goes next - probably back home for the same problems to recur. However he thought the boy's problems were psychological rather than financial as he had another boy from a middle class home with a similar problem of continuously running away from wherever he was placed.

Linda

Despite both team' interest in the research, they were in fact nervous about being observed in practice. Only Linda, one of the social work assistants, volunteered to take me out with her without further prompting on my part. She needed some help transporting some puppies to the RSPCA because the owners could not afford to keep them. As I got to know the social workers, it was easier to accompany and observe them in their day to day work without them feeling they had to make a special effort, or that they had to have different attitudes and actions in relation to poverty because a researcher was present. However despite the length of time spent with each team - nine months with Silverton and five months with City - there were occasions when I noticed social workers appearing to make comments for my benefit.

Participation in social work duties

The Silverton team had decided they did not want help with routine social work duties, because management might then be less likely to recognize the degree of under staffing and overwork there was in the team. Even so this study is defined as participant rather than non participant because there were many ways in which I did participate in both the Silverton and City teams. Participation included: giving and taking telephone messages; helping to transport furniture and clothes to social service users; supporting social workers who were dealing with child abuse problems and talking to them generally about their work which they appeared to find useful; being asked for opinions in team meetings and by individual social workers; putting up welfare rights information in the Silverton waiting room and supporting Brian the local welfare rights officer and Vernon the team leader, in organising social work meetings on welfare rights.

The effectiveness of the research in terms of policy and practice

Social workers in a social services team will not necessarily want to wait one or two years or longer to see the results of research on paper. They may have left social work, or moved on to specialise or promotion. Policy recommendations often involve resources which social services departments do not have, so how can they be implemented in practice?

It is extremely difficult for an individual researcher to have any lasting effect on policies on social work and poverty at the institutional level. The social services departments concerned had no motivation to carry out policy initiatives suggested, although they might find the results interesting. Furthermore the two social work teams concerned were structured in a particular way as a result of individual management and social services department policies. One researcher cannot be expected to have much of an impact.

In terms of action research, my presence as an observer prompted social workers to discuss how aware they were of the link between their attitudes and actions in relation to poverty. Furthermore in City Social Services a positive awareness of the poverty of social work users is supported by their policy documents. Vernon the Silverton teamleader arranged three meetings with welfare rights officers and the team. He checked that I would be there for the meetings, and he and Brian, the local welfare rights officer both admitted that prior to my arrival, there had not been a meeting for over six months. The meetings were concerning fuel debts, liaison with the welfare rights officers, and monies still available under community care grants. The Team leader also became aware that the local welfare rights officer wanted more support from social workers for the training he organises.

Research feedback

The two teams had somewhat different attitudes to the feedback sessions, which may reflect the different pressures they felt from the social services structure they were part of and the different areas they were working in.

Policy initiatives that would be constructive for the team as a whole were suggested and discussed. Assertiveness training provided by the researcher in the last month of the observation period was extremely useful in encouraging communication between myself, the team, and between team members and the team leader.

Both teams discussed feedback papers on the fieldwork which included policy initiatives that could be implemented by the team. From these taped debates, it appears that the initiatives that were accepted were ones that members of the team or the team leader had already discussed, but needed prompting into putting into practice. The policy suggestions that were not accepted were ones that seemed too radically different from the individual or team's way of working. (See Appendix 3)

Silverton team

The Silverton team worked in a rural area which also was statistically one of the poorest areas of that authority. However people applying to social services for financial help were limited because: there were fewer numbers living in the Silverton area, there were no huge high rise tower blocks as there were next door to the City offices; the settled rural nature of the community meant friends and relatives sometimes lived nearby and were more able to help; and the team had established with local social service users that they had a non cooperation policy with DSS on the Social Fund. Many of the social workers in the Silverton team were local women who tended to see a researcher as an 'expert'. They were therefore more likely to accept the suggested policy initiatives on paper if not in practice. They also seemed more upset by the suggestions that their attitudes and actions were not always consistent. These feelings were not expressed in the debate on the feedback paper, but to the team leader after I had left (See Appendix 3).

The team were keen to have a monthly problem session where they could bring up issues connected with poverty and welfare rights that were causing them problems. The welfare rights officers were to be invited, but the format suggested was task orientated and was more dependent on self help and the team working as a group, rather than the more formal welfare rights presentations I had observed during the fieldwork. This proposal was developing the concept of a poverty awareness programme with an informal structure where any issues connected with poverty could be discussed. Vernon however, was not keen on this policy initiative because he felt more meetings would take the social workers away from their work, when everyone was very stressed by the amount of work there was to do already.

The idea of having a permanent duty officer who had extra training on welfare rights, and a caseload that saw poverty issues as an area for detailed knowledge like other specialisms in social work, was not so well received because nobody wanted the job (see Appendix 3).

Carol: ... and then the idea that there should be a suggestion that maybe somebody should remain on duty to deal with poverty related or finance related queries (pause) um you know ugh!... the idea of doing that, that's not what I trained to do. I just wouldn't like the idea of doing that.

Since Carol's arrival in the team, during the last two months of the observation, she had been placed on the duty desk by the team leader, nearly every day, in order to get to know the type of problems that occurred in Silverton, and because social workers in both teams were not keen to take their turn on the duty desk. Carol may have felt some pressure to do other people's 'dirty work' and therefore reacted strongly to a suggestion from the research, that she might have felt would influence her future role in the team.

City team

The City team were situated in one of the poorest areas of the city, where there was high demand in terms of helping users with their financial problems. At the same time they were 'under siege' as their feedback paper was entitled, because their way of working under the patch system was not given the status they felt it deserved by the social services hierarchy. Consequently they tended to view the feedback paper as yet more criticism of their way of working when they had hoped it would show management how effective the patch system was. They also tended to be individuals who considered themselves 'progressive' and therefore felt they were already aware of the issues raised by the research.

The City team were defensive about feedback comments that I had not observed much welfare rights work in their practice. They denied that the welfare rights officers rather than social workers were dealing with these issues. They did not see the need for joint meetings with welfare rights officers from social services, nor did they think they were unaware of poverty issues. However a social work student who was on placement with the team whom I interviewed at her college, felt that the team were not always up to date with their welfare rights knowledge. She quoted an example of one of the social workers not realizing the benefit situation of a sixteen year old he was working with. The team leader who was not at the team meeting, but who I interviewed separately about the policy initiatives, wanted to initiate welfare rights sessions with the welfare rights officers. He said he had been thinking of doing this for some time but 'had not got round to it'. The City team already had on their agenda from their staff training day, the proposal that they should make representations to management concerning how their work output as a patch team was evaluated, and therefore this policy initiative from the research was accepted.

With the present squeeze on resources and changes to their ways of working, it is doubtful that either team will be particularly receptive to policy initiatives, unless they go some way to relieving the pressure on individual workers.

Conclusions

What methods have been most useful in fulfilling the initial theoretical interests outlined in the two tables, and what methods most suited the research topic? My experiences of quantitative and qualitative methodology have led to a critique of the rigid ways in which theory and method are linked, and the idea of purely objective methodology.

Having conducted a survey and organised group discussions and interviews, the thirteen month participant observation study led to the richest most meaningful data for a number of reasons. Theoretically emancipatory and practical interests have been to a great extent fulfilled using this method. From Fig 3.2, it appears that the methodological concerns best served have been in the practical sphere. However the critique employed would argue that boundaries are unrealistic between methodologies, and that within the participant observation methodology there have been examples of how emancipatory and technical as well as practical concerns have been highlighted.

The advantages of participant observation

Participant observation has the advantage of being longitudinal rather than 'snapshot' so there is the opportunity to reinforce some findings and conclusions while correlating or contrasting others. I do feel privileged to have been able to immerse myself in the fieldwork over 13 months in a way that is unlikely to be repeatable in terms of time and resources in a more established academic career. Furthermore field observation is interactive and dynamic, so that theory and method became integrated as new and interesting data promote exciting new ideas (see Figure 3.2). For example the feedback periods at the end of the observation period developed policy initiatives suggested by the researcher, but they were actively discussed by the participants rather than them being 'objects' of the research. Participant observation proved an effective method in which to gain 'subject' to 'subject' interaction. The fieldwork methodology also 'fitted' the research question. I was interested in establishing how social workers' attitudes to poverty could be understood in relation to their actions. Very few other methods allow the researcher to record and observe attitudes and also observe actions. Without a familiarity with the subjects of the study and the environment over time, it would be impossible to assess whether such attitudes and actions were contrived for the researcher. Burgess (1988) has argued that the capacity of the ethnographic project 'to surprise us' is its greatest strength and Bastin (1985) suggests observation is a method that is greatly under utilized as a contribution to policy planning. It is particularly applicable where changes, such as the Social Fund, are likely to have a direct influence on peoples' lives.

Fieldwork studies

Although there have been fieldwork studies of professional groups such as the police, the military, and many with teachers, there have been surprisingly few with social workers (Johnson 1975, Mathinson and Sinclair 1979, Satyamurti 1981, Pithouse 1987) and none that are solely concerned with attitudes and actions in relation to poverty.

Becker (1997, p.549) suggests further qualitative research on social work and poverty is needed:

> Until social work, their managers and agencies understand how poverty impacts upon clients and how attitudes, structures and contradictions affect the nature and delivery of social work services, then it is unlikely that the poor will receive a service that is appropriate to their needs.

Participant observation offered a surprising, realistic and valuable method with which to understand how poverty impacts on clients, and what role social workers play in this process. Field observation may be equally useful for similar studies which seek to discover how individuals translate attitudes into actions and appears relatively unacknowledged as a research methodology that can lead to action research and the development of policy initiatives.

4 Social work students and social work education

This chapter asks how do social work students come to know and attach meaning to the theory and practice they learn on their courses. It is suggested that social work students do assimilate theory, but are not able to integrate theory and practice sufficiently on their social work courses.

Data from four group discussions with 59 social work students from Sheffield University and Sheffield Hallam University and quantitative information from a pilot study survey of thirty nine social work students at three further universities - Middlesex, Hertfordshire and NE London are also included.

How do social work students come to know and learn?

> Sorcerers say that we are inside a bubble. It is a bubble into which we are placed at the moment of our birth. At first the bubble is open, but then it begins to close until it has sealed us in. That bubble is our perception. We live inside that bubble all of our lives. And what we witness on its round walls is our own reflection (Castaneda 1973, p.43).

What social work students come to know on a social work course will be a product of their individual perception, influenced by: their background and past experiences, the institutional and teaching ideology of the educational establishment, their course and their practice placements, and the peer group with whom they are training. What they think they have learnt may change again once they are practising social work (Freed 1995). Educationalists and philosophers have explored different kinds of 'knowing'. They distinguish between objective, analytic, verifiable external knowledge and inner knowledge based on subjective, divergent or intuitive perceptions.

While evidence can usually be produced for external knowledge, inner knowledge can merge so well with the beliefs of 'the person who knows', that it is difficult to verify. 'I know that I am aware of poverty in my work, and my attitudes and actions reflect this awareness', is harder to evaluate than 'I know what benefits are available from the DSS for a one parent family'.

Social work students discuss objective knowledge as external, and academic while internal subjective knowledge is related to their own personal beliefs and social work practice.

> Martin: I think also in the lectures and things we've examined things like the structural causes of poverty,... which I think is really good. But ... that's something that's never been related to actual social work practice...obviously if you're interested in it you'll do that anyway and for me that's what I think all my social work practice was about. But I think it's very easy to see structural causes as somewhere in academia...which has not got much to do with social work. And maybe seeing family therapy and counselling... as something that's really social work. And it's been split, ...there hasn't been that much integration of how the structural causes of poverty should affect social work practice (Hallam University, Group One).

Sheffield University students had a similar perspective.

> Mary:..there's very little opportunity in the course itself to bring the experience and the theory together in any kind of meaningful way...

> Gina: I think we've had opportunities as well to do sort of individual pieces of work haven't we that can touch on poverty? But again that's from a very theoretical perspective, there hasn't been a chance to really touch on that sense of personal hopelessness that you have in some situations when you feel that you can do almost nothing, how do you cope with that? (Sheffield University, Group One).

Surrounding this issue are concerns which question how students attach meaning to their learning (Dean and Fleck 1992), what they need to know (Pearson 1975), and whether there is sufficient time in the overloaded social work curriculum for students to know about anything in depth (Howe 1989).

Research on social work education

Gardiner (1988, p.4) is critical of much research on social work education:

> It is of enduring curiosity to me that social work educators frequently talk about learning, but go on to describe the content of teaching or the content of assessment - without giving much attention to *how* students learn.

How social work students see and construe their world and the way this influences learning is the constructivist perspective adopted in this chapter. Such an approach examines how social work students construct and resolve social work issues based on their own perceptions of others' views and behaviours.

Understanding how students learn is not a particularly new approach in that studies from Sweden in the mid 1970s (cited in Gardiner and Matthias 1988) refocused educational research by looking at learning from the consumer's perspective. What is learned and how that learning occurs is investigated, rather than measuring how much is learned, or what it will cost, as in behavioural and evaluation research on education.

The major finding of this approach to educational research is that students learn in different ways. As Howe (1989, p.11) notes, 'It now seems well established that the more overloaded is the curriculum, the more likely it is that students will resort to surface reproductive learning'. Social work students in the postgraduate groups felt that the pressure of course work was hindering them from exploring the nature and meaning of social work generally, but also specifically in relation to the relationship between poverty and social work.

> Margaret:...you're too busy writing the essays to make sure it'll pass to think the issue through, so you've read a couple of chapters from the book, but you haven't read it and *you don't know* and you don't have the time to think it through. (Mm from others)...there's so much pressure on this course to write essays, to do this, to do the other but there isn't time to integrate that kind of learning, and it isn't done and I think its a big lack (Sheffield University, Group One).

Criticisms of this deep/surface approach to learning would suggest that the student's own interests, attitudes and ideology will affect what she studies in depth and understands the meaning of, and what she strategically applies a surface approach to.

> Fiona: ...I think you could have actually got through the course and still

do that if you weren't interested in poverty. You could get through this course and not have any idea about it, it could wash over you (Hallam University, Group Two).

Furthermore students may, for personal reasons unconnected with education, adopt a deep approach in one particular time and place but not in another. However Entwistle (1987) suggests a deep approach can increase understanding and use of the concepts learned after a course has been completed. Such an approach is therefore particularly relevant for a vocational course where unlike for example a zoology graduate who becomes a management trainee, students must utilise what they have learnt in their future work.

What have we learnt so far about social work education?

Educational research can evaluate teaching and learning in: ideological, moral and normative terms, quantitative, behavioural and economic terms, and qualitative, experiential and subjective terms. Howe (1989, p.17) suggests the following future for the research debate on what and how social work students learn:

> Combining the recommendations of practice evaluators and training evaluators, we can pick out a number of common, and therefore key words - small scale, collaborative, participative, learner's perspective, client's view, exploratory. Weave these together and we begin to have some useful ideas about how to move forward on both educational and practical fronts.

Social work is an occupation that requires a multitude of personal qualities as well as specific knowledge (Abell and McDonnel 1990). There is a danger that only that which can be measured will be taught, so that the tools of the behavioural researcher define the curriculum and ultimately the practice of social work. For example the parts of welfare rights that could be tested would be taught but not poverty awareness. Social workers may be aware they have been trained adequately in welfare rights but they may not be aware of the prejudices they have towards people who are poor.

What social work students or social workers feel they need to know may not be what CCETSW, local authorities or social service users feel they need to know or what research commissioned by any number of interested groups, suggests they need to know. The problem is often ideological - who is evaluating the educational process and what their interests are. For example students may be very appreciative of a poverty awareness programme, but social work managers may claim that this did not lead to effective practice. Users of social services on the other hand may be pleased with what the students have to offer. Reversing the scenario, students may not be satisfied with course content or teaching style, and yet employers and users are satisfied.

Who controls social work education is a key question. Howe (1989) suggests social service users, as consumers, should evaluate student social workers and by implication have an impact on the social work curriculum. Lyons (1992) proposes a consideration of human rights in relation to social service users' rights relative to the power and resources of professionals. This could facilitate a stronger direction for incorporation of users' views in the assessment and evaluation of social work courses. Parsloe (1990) in *Social Work Education in the Year 2000*, would wish to broaden the scope of social work education to enable social workers to develop partnerships with users, members of other social disciplines, politicians and theoreticians so that students have a broader based understanding of individual problems which may mitigate social worker burnout.

Education and training and the evaluation of education and training, involve competing ideologies, resources and power bases. Poverty awareness training for example may only be accepted by some individuals in professional and lay groups. However such a programme is a way forward in teaching and learning about poverty, and is a response not only to Parsloe's emphasis on students' understanding of their own values and the structural nature of poverty but also Dean and Fleck's (1992) dilemma. They suggest that the challenge for the constructivist in social work education, lies in finding ways to address the realities of poverty, oppression and power while honouring individual constructions of these conditions.

What is professional knowledge?

A body of knowledge has been developed that refers to the particular activities defined as social work. There will further be a collection of recipes that must be learned if the student is to perform social work 'correctly'. This knowledge serves as a channelling controlling force in itself and an essential ingredient of the institutionalization of this area of work (Berger and Luckman 1967).

To 'do' social work and be a social worker imply existence in a social world defined and controlled by this body of knowledge. So for example, a student practice teacher who wanted to supervise social work students in her community work setting found that the language and terms used on the practice teacher course were alien to her and her background of community work education, even though one would have assumed they had similar professional roots. The sociology of knowledge leads us to the conclusion that every profession has a body of professional knowledge. Such knowledge may be wide ranging and open to discussion, it is unlikely to be static or fixed.

The origins of social work as a profession, suggest that initially, social workers' knowledge was assumed to be concerned with the deserving and undeserving poor. This knowledge was assimilated within a knowledge of psychodynamics and psychology in order to establish the connection between psychiatry, medicine and social work (see Chapter 1). However Howe (1989, p.16) notes there is a trend towards management techniques as the knowledge base for social work:

> The penchant of trainers and employers for practices which are task centred, time specific and target-orientated may say more about accountability and measurement in the welfare services than the practice of good social work.

Jordan (1987) and Abell and Mcdonnel (1990) argue that integrating personal and professional experiences of social work and understanding users' views are crucial elements of social work knowledge.

> ...social workers should be taught as much about how to understand what is personally meaningful to their clients, as what is generally acceptable in various spheres of society... creativity and imagination may be as important for good social work as thoroughness and order (Jordan 1987, p.144).

What is considered social work knowledge has changed over time, though such knowledge is institutionalised in the sense that 'new' knowledge, such as welfare rights, has difficulty becoming an accepted part of the social work curriculum (Mcgrail 1983).

> Joanne: Don't you think there's been quite a good input on welfare rights?...I think its actually down to one person that fought very hard at getting a big chunk of our second year on welfare rights (Hallam University, Group One).

Later on in the same discussion, one student admitted he had difficulty getting his tutors to accept a welfare rights advice centre as his final placement:

> Interviewer: Do you think that college tutors have a particular attitude toward poverty, welfare rights...?

> Michael: I think one of the things which probably sums up their attitude is the fact that for me doing a final placement at a welfare rights and advice place, there was a hell of a lot of tutors here who felt that wasn't appropriate for a social worker, that they didn't feel that welfare rights or campaign work was part of social work. Now obviously the people who did this welfare rights course wouldn't have thought that, but I mean that sort of runs through, and I had to fight quite hard to get that placement.
>
> Interviewer: Is that particular tutors or ...a general feeling that you met?
>
> Michael: ...I'd say there was a split, probably half or more would say that (the welfare rights placement) wasn't a social work experience.

Is there one 'body' of social work knowledge? Gardiner's (1988 and 1989) research on learning suggests there is no one perspective on social work which encompasses all that students need to know. His evaluation of social work supervision suggests that students learn most effectively and permanently by an interactive process. However his proposition that the 'best' form of learning is that which integrates different perspectives on social work is not one with which all would agree. Some philosophers, academics and practitioners would wish to understand and consider the world from one perspective. This student for example, seems to have adopted an approach that deliberately concentrates on a definition of social work that is concerned with material need.

> Interviewer: Do you feel very confident that you understand the relationship between poverty and social work, do you feel that's been an area you're fairly to grips with in terms of what you've been taught on the course? Is it something you see as important or not important?
>
> Martin: For me I feel it's quite high but ...nearly every essay I've done I've managed to sort of choose essays which concentrate on it. When it comes to it that's my interest anyway and I have got a lot out of the course on that, because that's probably the only area where I've actually done any reading. I have become more knowledgeable - yes (Hallam University, Group Two).

However integration of the different parts of what is considered social work knowledge is crucial to learning according to most of the social work students:

> Mary: I think it's really difficult because in a lot of ways on our course

we've had it in different compartments, so we've had our social policy lectures and we've tackled poverty from that point of view. We've had our social work lectures and we've tackled emotional deprivation on that perspective, but there's been very little opportunity to bring those two things together and to see it in any overall sense. And that's a sort of rolling problem because as we experience this kind of stuff first hand which we're still doing obviously at the moment, then there's no opportunity to integrate those experiences into the stuff we had in the first year. So in a way if we are integrating them, we're doing it in our own heads, and personally I feel I'm lagging behind and I'm struggling with it to sort of bring it altogether. There's very little opportunity in the course itself to bring the experience and the theory together in any kind of meaningful way (Sheffield University, Group One).

The student who is trying to personally understand her social work knowledge may be dealing with the contradictory and confusing nature of that knowledge. The problem is not necessarily hers but the dilemma of whether conflicting theories can be reconciled into a recognisable body of social work knowledge. The difficulty of integrating different aspects of social work knowledge for many social work students in their group discussions and questionnaires could be a symptom of the complicated task of defining social work and social work knowledge, and hence social work as a profession (Pearson 1973, Dowling 1986, Dean and Fleck 1992).

The relationship between theory and practice

This is a complex relationship in a number of ways. Students may assimilate and understand theory and its integration with practice more clearly when they evaluate their course after they have completed it and are practising social work. Although one would want to foster a thorough approach to learning and to encourage the integration of theory with practice, whatever the theory, it may be that such an approach leads to irreconcilable differences between for example psychodynamic and sociological theories on poverty.

Barbour's (1984) study implies social work students have a superficial approach to all theory and only use it to explain their practice when forced to do so. Students were required to produce a 'situational study' based on practice placements and 'could be overheard discussing... what 'names' they could give to their methods of working with clients' (p.569). He cynically suggests a 'subconscious assimilation' theory for students and practitioners who say they have assimilated theory 'subconsciously' into their practice!

In this study, it appeared that some students had a thorough rather than 'subconscious' understanding of the relationship between theories on poverty, welfare rights knowledge, and social work practice. While they may have had such knowledge before embarking on their course, it seems likely that they *have* gained knowledge from academic teaching and placement experience. In all four group discussions, the social work students stressed the need for theory and practice to be more integrated.

> Theresa: I think Martin hit it on the head when he said about the integration bit because personally I think there's still that sort of mismatch.
>
> Interviewer: Are you thinking particularly with poverty and social work or are you thinking that's a general problem?
>
> Theresa: I think it's a general problem as well but in particular for poverty and social work I think... we had quite a lot about poverty and social work in various guises on the course over the two years ...but it seems to suddenly come to a dead end really, and we went out on final practice and there were all these issues going on and all these things going through parliament and there was a divide that needed to be filled by something.
>
> Sarah: There was also an expectation that that would be provided on our practice placement without that being enabled to happen,... the responsibility for that integration doesn't happen here, ... its left as being out there...we're missing out because it's so hit and miss. (Hallam University, Group One).

Lorna felt that theory/practice integration was only part of the story.

> Interviewer: So it's having some support in a personal sense as well as being able to integrate theory with practice, it's having a sort of feeling of...?
>
> Lorna: Not exactly support because that to me suggests something external but there's something in our future working lives that we're going to have to cope with on a day to day basis, so it's learning those coping mechanisms really and how you deal with that personally,...All those sorts of issues which we may have dealt with in the first year a bit like in social policy, but actually for me anyway they are coming up all the time and as my experience changes then my perspective on it

changes too (Sheffield University, Group One).

Where integration of theory and practice was successful, students' confidence in their practice and beliefs had developed accordingly.

> Interviewer: So you feel more competent than you did before you came?
>
> Maurice: I've got more sort of basis to what I felt before I came.
>
> Interviewer: What about other people?
>
> Sheila: I think I would echo that as well, I think I've been more able to argue in a more constructive way and not from what you feel about the relationship between race, class, gender, and poverty and social work in particular. ... I think I've used the course to search out and follow up bits of reading as well and incorporate things in my essays and I think, I've now got a much sounder base on which I can base arguments.
>
> Janet: I think its done that for me really, before I came on the course I knew poverty was always a major issue because of the kind of work I've done before, but yes it's done that for me given me a bit more confidence really, sounder knowledge and more of a base from which to argue.
>
> Interviewer: Is that fairly general?
>
> Mm (general agreement)
>
> Helen: I think as far as the exercising of regulations, I felt more confident before because of practice, but now I have a greater confidence I think on the understanding of the underlying stuff, the implications strategies, than I did before the course (Hallam University, Group One).

Generally the research findings indicate that social work students do appear to have gained theoretical knowledge during their social work courses, and in some cases integrated it successfully with their social work practice, thus giving them more confidence for their future practice. However the extent of the theory/practice integration and whether it remains important in work is not clear.

Conclusions

What has been established about what social work students know, how they know and what meaning is attached to what they know? It has been suggested that: students 'make sense' of their knowledge, give it meaning, according to the location, structures, situations, and actors that are present at the time; that a body of 'professional' knowledge develops as a way of legitimating the social work profession in society, but that knowledge will change with time, ideologies, and individual circumstances. It has also been suggested that students learn in different ways, which will be mediated by their: attitudes, actions and educational and personal environment.

Students who participated in the group discussions and completed questionnaires felt that poverty and welfare rights and their relationship to social work were important issues and were not sufficiently well addressed on their courses or in their placements. They were particularly concerned that theory was not sufficiently integrated with practice.

Although students in group discussions and on the questionnaires were critical of teaching on poverty, welfare rights and social work, they also had many constructive comments to make about how their learning and knowledge could be improved in relation to these subjects. As consumers of the education service and as observers of a social work service, their comments and suggestions need to be taken seriously.

Students' expectations of their courses may be unrealistic. As one student said, 'the course is too short to fit everything in you need to'. CCETSW's long list of requirements for those completing a social work course would support this statement. Courses have enormous pressure on them to deliver social work knowledge in terms of: depth, competing subject areas, and course structures and modules. Teaching staff may find it difficult to adapt to a different way of teaching or new knowledge, and/or there may not be resources to buy in guest speakers, or other teaching aids that may be necessary.

Nevertheless there has been a long standing neglect of poverty issues on social work courses in the UK, the USA, Canada, Australia, Bulgaria and developing countries (Parsloe, 1990, Lyons 1992, Tully 1994, Ryan 1992, Lord 1992, Freed 1995, Larochelle and Campfens 1992, Quiroz 1992). A greater percentage of users are poor than they are female, disabled, black, young or old. This is not to suggest that these groupings are not important, but that poverty is likely to be an overall difficulty that affects all user groups (Campfens 1992, Becker 1997). Social work students need to be aware of poverty in the same way that they are expected to be aware of race, sex and class discrimination. The next chapter examines students' perceptions of poverty issues on social work placements and in their previous work settings and suggest a poverty awareness programme that can be developed by social work educators.

5 Social work students' attitudes to poverty

This chapter utilises a constructionist approach to the qualitative data to examine in detail social work students' attitudes to the relationship between poverty and social work, and to the role of welfare benefits in social work. What social work students, as observers of social work practice, have to say about social work placements and previous work settings is valuable evidence to set alongside the participant observation findings. A poverty awareness programme is presented as one solution to the evidence of dissatisfactions of social work students in chapters four and five regarding teaching on social work and poverty.

Students' views on the relationship between poverty and social work

A number of the examples given by students showed the extreme financial hardship facing social service users.

> Martin: I'm thinking of one client I had ...I remember going in to see him, and came out almost in tears because I went in to see a man whose wife was due to have a baby in about six weeks and all they had was just a broken down radiogram in the corner and they both just sat there in the freezing cold, trying to keep themselves together. It made me wonder what ever we were about. There was very little I could do for these people, they'd had a grant about a year previously so they couldn't get another one and they were in a pretty bad state. I tried to raise them up with the agency but it was impossible, they don't have money for that kind of thing. I then had to go to several charities to try

and get money and things. And it seems that social work hasn't got away from that over the years, its very beginning was to turn to charities and they still remain to an extent handing out things to people ...and we perpetuate it by the fact that I was able to go out and beg and got stuff for this couple. When they eventually got another visit from the DSS, they'd got new carpets in, they'd got the fridge and they'd got various things so they were not in need, they didn't need these things so they didn't get. When we're doing things like going begging ...rather than saying to the State, 'look you know this isn't on, we can't have some people living in squalor like this and have to rely on what other people don't want really' (Hallam University, Group Two).

As far as how social service users' financial situation impinged on their work, Jan echoed comments made by the two social work teams in the fieldwork,

Jan: You asked the question of thinking of specific examples of people in poverty and the problems they faced...it's actually hard to think of specific examples, because you just come across it all the time...if you start to think of specific examples, my mind goes into things like the needy, the really, really needy and I don't think you should go into that. It's like it's just there. (Hallam University, Group One).

All of the students in the group discussions at Hallam University and Sheffield University could give examples of problems they had to deal with in relation to poverty. All thirty nine of the social work students in the pilot study at three other Universities told of similar experience in their placements.

Some of the students in one of the university groups implied poor users had little power to help themselves. Margaret discusses this woman's situation as part of a large extended family, who had also received help from the Family Services Unit (FSU), over an extended period.

Margaret: I had never before been into a house quite as bad as this one. I had been into many that were very rough but they had nearly nothing in their house - I mean the smell of urine was all the way through it, with the kids who even at ten and twelve were wetting the bed every night. She didn't have things in a financial or material sense which was important to her but she also didn't have something in herself to overcome some of these things that were just dragging them all down. I'll never forget the day she actually came to me, to the FSU which is across the dual carriageway from the other side of town and that she'd actually walked across roads to do this - admittedly she'd kept one of her children with her to do it but that she'd done it ... (University, Group One).

In one sense Margaret felt her client from FSU was 'deserving' in that she had made the effort to cross the road to come and see her, but in another sense she felt she could not be helped,

> Interviewer: If she'd been OK financially do you think that emotional deprivation would still have been there?
>
> Margaret: Yes from what I know of her background. Financial or material things were important to her but ... her boyfriend one Christmas he won something gambling, he won the races - he won a lot of money - the kids got some very expensive presents, an expensive bike, but they didn't really care for them and in a sense it meant nothing. The things got damaged very quickly, one of the bikes got lost. Eventually it got returned but it was something to do with emotional poverty that said that you could have poured financial stuff in from here to kingdom come but unless you did something about some of the other side of things it wasn't going to end. That's not to say that the financial or material poverty wasn't important, but they were only part of the picture.

Margaret's perspective on this family's poverty seems to indicate that their problem is part of a cycle of deprivation, is psychological and can only be resolved by individual counselling. Townsend's (1979 p.70) comment on Oscar Lewis' (1966) work could equally be applied as a way of thinking from some social workers which appears to depend on valuing the concept of the 'underclass' (Murray 1990).

> He (Oscar Lewis) may have helped even if unwittingly to divert interest ...in solutions to poverty away from economic and social reconstruction to individual training and character reform, from costly redistributive policies to low cost social work and community psychiatry.

There was a tendency in one particular postgraduate student group to identify poverty as 'emotional deprivation' from which there was no escape. Parsloe (1990) notes that while it is essential that social work students are educated on the structural nature of poverty, they need to retain an awareness that the poor also suffer the same sorrows as the rich. But those in poverty do have additional burdens to bear that would cause stress and worry to the better off if their circumstances were reversed.

> Mary: Something that strikes me is the sort of general state of mind of a lot of the clients that have been oppressed by poverty, in that they don't really have any hope of getting out of where they are...All of us from our sort of privileged backgrounds, we can all kind of see various alternatives and lifestyles and we can actually choose those, but the people that we're actually dealing with in our work are sort of stuck at a level and they don't really see any options. And I feel that it would be much easier to deal with people who had more options available to them, they could actually see there were these things so that there was more sort of potential for personal change (University, Group One).

Some students labelled families as 'passive' while other students described aggressive acts as a reaction to an intolerable situation. Jennifer described how a couple who were living in bed and breakfast with their child, needed money for disposable nappies - they had nowhere to wash ordinary ones. They were told by DSS that they could have no more money. They broke a window at the offices and were prosecuted for criminal damage. This involved paying more fines. Hopelessness and depression turned to frustration and anger.

Previous experience

Some students remembered previous social work practice experiences to explain their definition of the relationship between poverty and social work. Fran's experience of living on a low income was unusual and positive in helping her to understand social service users' perspective.

> Fran: I think as well when you experience it (poverty) ... before I came on the course I was a 'home-maker' which meant that I had to actually go and live in the home with exactly the same amount of money in exactly the same circumstances ... you know its temporary ... and that I think it brings home to you very much in practice (Hallam University, Group Two).

Whereas Marilyn's previous experience within social services was more negative,

> Marilyn: I worked in a social services department as a social work assistant for three years and to try and keep the leaflets up to date, to try to keep people (social services staff) even slightly interested or even want to look at the CPAG handbooks was quite a major achievement

really. ... and consistently on duty you would get social workers give out really bad welfare rights advice... they had a training course about three years earlier and they'd say 'oh you've got four hundred quid savings oh well you can't apply for a single payment' (for single parents)... even though the cut off level had gone up to five hundred. They just weren't keeping up to date with the changes basically, giving people bad advice and those were the people who actually wanted to do welfare rights work. Quite a lot of social workers don't see welfare rights work or the issue of poverty as their work at all, which is very worrying to say the least (Hallam University, Group One).

Social control and non intervention

The Hallam University groups were concerned that the relationship between poverty and social work was one where the defining element in relation to social service users was one of social control.

> Interviewer: What about the relationship between poverty and social work what is the relationship at the moment do you think?
>
> Janet: Sticking plaster, we act as sticking plasters without actually tackling and doing something.
>
> Michael: In a sense social work helps people cope better with a really bad situation and will not change that situation in any real way.
>
> Janet: And will not challenge that.
>
> Interviewer: Do you think social work could do that or do you think its impossible anyway?
>
> Janet: I think you've got to actually to look at the fact of social work as an institution and see where social work as an institution lies politically and in society and the structure of society and we are there specifically for that purpose to keep the lid on things...then social work in some ways is quite unacceptable to me - but then you've then got to actually balance that off with the individual work that you do and you get caught in that and that's how the cog continues. But I suppose you've just got to look at the fact that the biggie at the moment is sexual abuse, the fact that we're busy round council houses rushing in all their kids but we're not knocking on doors in Darwin and Tithe

(middle class areas). The whole thing about that is the dysfunctional family, the working class family that can't cope and ...we're busy policing there but we're not actually doing anything about middle class abuse of their children (Hallam University, Group One).

Giving and withholding money was seen by some students as part of the state's and the individual social worker's system of social control.

Malcolm: The thing is we all know that poverty is a major part of our work. But what frightens me is the way it's used in social work, in that often the way we work with people, giving money from Section 17, or for people to pursue their claim..it does make you feel as though you're helping the person who is coming. But it's used as a tool to almost get them on your side, to work in other sorts of ways with people... (Hallam University, Group Two).

Not being needed and not having power was a problem too.

Sylvia: You can't get away from the fact that when you do provide, get extra money for somebody like if you get them attendance allowance that's been refused ...you do put twenty or thirty quid a week in that household and you disappear. You're not really in, you're not as important... And also that continues to trap you in working with individuals (Hallam University, Group One).

One student suggested that social workers should refuse to give social service users money, as a way of pressurising the state to take on this responsibility, and to avoid the danger of perhaps enjoying that personal power - other students disagreed.

Interviewer: If you had a chance to reorganise social work, you know everything else is the same, still got the Social Fund, still got the Social Security Act, what ideally would you like social workers to be doing in relation to poverty?

Michael: I think social workers ought ...to effectively fight poverty and that would mean taking on their own bosses. I think community workers for example are ...encouraged to take on their own bosses whereas social workers are not encouraged to do so. And I think it's because you have to pay attention to your caseload and it's essentially about casework so the will would have to be there for all social workers to want to change the way in which they work. I think the most effective thing I can see is what's been mentioned as radical non-intervention, don't do anything,...to me the primary role of social work is social control, and therefore if you're not doing social control then the state will have to take perhaps notice of people and of their plight.

Interviewer: So if somebody comes to you and says they've got no money, you don't do anything? Does everybody agree with that?

Ruth: No, I agree with the idea but just to sit there and say to somebody whose sat in front of me 'OK I can't do anything about ...'

Michael: Say, 'go to your MP go and hassle your MP'.

Ruth: Say that as well don't you? I mean if you just say 'I can't help you' a lot of people will just be accepting that and go away and not do anything else.

Jane: That's the dilemma that you're in all the time isn't it? How can you change things whilst not letting those people coming to you at the moment suffer more than they need to? Does a whole generation or whatever it is, of individuals have to suffer for what will eventually be the common good, I don't know.

By the end of the group discussion, Michael appeared to have changed his mind about a policy of radical non intervention. Instead he appeared to be advocating welfare benefits advice and advocacy rather than income maintenance.

Interviewer: . ..So one alternative would be to not do anything, and the other alternative would be to get as much as possible? Any other views on that?

Michael: I think that's what social workers are doing and what probation people have done is to seek to get as much for the client simply because the next time round the government might be encouraged then to provide more money... I think if we don't make full use of what is available, then the government might take the view that the need is not as great ...and provide even less money but that goes against all that I've been saying before about propping up the system, but when you're actually faced with the reality. I mean one is about what happens in an ideal world and one is about what happens in reality and the reality when somebody says 'My giro hasn't come' or whatever it is, then that's what you respond to (Hallam University, Group Two).

Women and poverty

Many of the stories of poverty given by the student groups concerned women. Joanne had an awareness of why this mother was generally depressed and apathetic.

> Joanne: I worked with a twenty two year old, single mother left on her own,...the father of the children had basically taken the money and used it, taken the furniture, flogged it, so leaving her in a very depressed state, but also materially with very little and a number of debts. The stage where I became involved, she'd been placed on probation with the whole situation hanging over her and with deductions from her Income Support taken at source (for fuel bills)...This left her in a position of very little money in her hand or not enough. I mean there wasn't enough to clothe the kids, for her to look after herself properly, resulting in her denying herself sufficient food to feed the kids properly, leaving her who was already low and demoralised even more so, by not getting the basic nutrition that she needed.
>
> Interviewer: This was a probation case was it?
>
> Joanne: Yes
>
> Interviewer: How were you involved in it?
>
> Joanne: She was placed on probation for having stolen a bottle of Bacardi around Christmas time. I think she was principally put on probation because of the welfare considerations rather than the offence... (Hallam University, Group One).

The probation students in this group did not comment directly on the gendered nature of sentencing policies for men and women (Smart and Smart 1978). However Janet and Sandra suggested stealing a bottle of Bacardi would be likely to be looked on unfavourably by the courts and would label the individual as 'undeserving' poor. Would a man, stealing a bottle of Bacardi be similarly stigmatised? Other crimes connected with poverty committed by women have a more 'deserving' label.

> Janet: If she'd stolen two pairs of knickers for her daughters, she'd

probably be looked on alright by the court...I think a lot of them have got this attitude...they're full of pity for the poor and everything else, and that's not the magistrates, that's some probation officers.

Sandra: There's a bit of a danger to think of these people doing social work and probation as part of social work history...because I think the courses around produce people with those attitudes as well... (Hallam University, Group One).

This second account shows little awareness by social services of the practical problems of bringing up children alone where financial issues complicate a difficult situation (Gregory 1991).

Jan: There was a woman in recently, single parent again, having problems with a cooker and all sorts of things, it's like the usual tale. She was wanting a Section 17 payment over the difficult period, and because she'd had previous payments, was therefore deemed less needy or less worthy. She'd been a bit of a regular at the door so Division X said that she would have to come in everyday for her two pounds for five days. Two pounds per day per child so that was four pounds per day she was coming in for, because she had two children. But her bus fares including her children, were coming up to something like eighty pence so she was actually going away with a pittance and having to come back everyday. By the Friday, she was absolutely at the end of her tether and her kids were driving her barmy. There were a couple of Principals on the Division who had a very punitive attitude to people who wanted Section 17 relief and she threw a wobbler on the Division and was thrown out of the building. You know, it's just like the frustration had just transferred into a load of anger and violence, ...not actually physical violence against the social workers but it was put it in the violence at work book and we all talked about it and she was labelled even further. That woman was just treated badly by everybody. I mean of the sixteen last incidents, this is of violence on Division X social services, something like thirteen of them were in the office, and nine of those were refusals of Section 17 money, that's a direct link with poverty (Hallam University, Group Two).

What is most troubling about this account is that the social services personnel involved do not seem aware of the process by which the single parent concerned feels she has to earn her right to be seen as 'deserving' poor. By losing her temper she is then labelled 'undeserving', difficult and demanding. From the evidence in the 'violence at work' book it appears there were other individuals who, already faced with the stigma of poverty and having to ask for money, were further rejected by not feeling they were 'deserving enough' to receive Section 17 monies. Chapter seven describes a similar incident in the fieldwork where the couple - Mr and Mrs Baker appear to social workers as aggressive and demanding rather than passive and grateful. Polakow's (1994) qualitative study of poor women and children in Michigan, USA noted that welfare reform as exemplified by Michigan social services was punitive towards single mothers and children and that a 'carrot and stick' approach contributed little towards a viable family life.

Social work placements

Many of the students encountered financial deprivation for the first time on placement. They were distressed because rather than being in control and able to help their clients, they felt demeaned by the actions they took in relation to the client's poverty. Mary's account illustrates this conflict.

> Mary: Well I've just started on placement and she'd (Mrs Jones) told me this incredibly long complicated story about her family problems. At the end of it I said, 'Well do you want me to come and see you and what are we going to work on?' And she wasn't interested in working on any of these problems because she had no food for the week-end, because they'd given her double money at the post office two weeks before because it had been a bank holiday - she wasn't able to budget sufficiently, 'cos she'd got fines for this, that and the other and so now she hadn't got any food for the weekend right? I was there on a Thursday, she said 'Can I get some money from Family and Community Services?' so I said, 'Well I don't know' because they'd already refused her a few weeks before, 'cos they're cutting down on Section 17 money in that division and I knew that the Family Service Unit didn't have any money to give out - but there was a possibility of food parcels...Because it was my first interview with her, I didn't know whether this was appropriate so I couldn't assure her that she was going to get some food for the weekend from me - she couldn't get money from her family, or friends or relations because they're all in exactly the same position. Now having had this experience of going into this house which was filthy, the clothes were poor and everything was run down about it, I walked into town I went to the building society because I just happened to have my grant and I was putting some of my money into the building society and I walked into the building society with a cheque for £500 of my money to put into the

> building society. And the contrast between that woman and the physical conditions of her life, the fact that she had no food for the weekend I walked through town and there was all these people walking around buying things, putting money into the building society, standing there well dressed with gold jewellery on - all the rest of it. I made her a food parcel which I took back the next morning and I felt demeaned having to do it, and that it was demeaning to her that I chose what she was going to eat that weekend. That was all I could do and it was better than nothing because if I didn't do it she would have nothing to eat. But the sheer contrast between her life and the lives of everybody else, and the contrast between her life and my life and I'm a student and I'm fairly poor but like the quantity of poverty that she's up against... (University, Group One).

In situations of this sort, it is no wonder that social workers either become immune to the financial distress of users or adopt a fatalistic approach and feel there is nothing they can do. Many social work agencies have little money or other practical help to give poor users, and it seems unlikely that Mrs Jones would be entitled to additional DSS payments, although Mary did not mention whether she carried out a benefits check with her.

Some students could give positive accounts of how their placement agency dealt with financial issues.

> Sarah: I worked with an agency that deals with elderly people and they were very efficient in dealing with the system...They actually had a welfare rights adviser and a volunteer who was from the citizens advice bureau who was able to discuss with them (social service users), all the rights and the changes in benefits. We had twenty five people in day care four days a week and they interviewed everyone individually before the new (DSS) system came in, went over the benefits and filled the correct forms in...,so when it came in they were able to be fair and comfortable...it was well thought out and well planned and organised (Hallam University, Group Two).

If a social work placement in a day centre can organise a rights based approach to financial issues, there seems no reason why most social work agencies could not do the same, if they were convinced that dealing with money was part of the agency's and/or social work's remit. Unfortunately many more of the examples from students were of social work agencies who did not deal adequately with poverty issues or were unprepared for social security changes.

> Fiona: My placement was at the hospital... there was lots of confusion as to what was happening (regarding social security changes). Social workers all had different ideas, some of them had been trained, some had some training, some hadn't had any at all and various situations would crop up with patients. Often social workers would come back to the social work department to try and speak to other people who might know something about it or find out, there was just a lot of confusion going on (Hallam University, Group Two).

> John: I mean in the advice centre the number of people who came in who had social workers and they were not getting the right benefit, to me, that just seems ridiculous. I mean that's one of the first things you can do for somebody at least, sort out their benefits and make sure that they're getting what they're entitled to, but time and time and again people came in who'd had social workers for ten years who never even touched on that side of things (Hallam University, Group One).

Students were however concerned that advising users about the Social Fund meant that they were either helping people to get into debt if a loan was involved or depriving those claimants who were not social service users, but may be more in need, if the application was for a grant.

> Kate: The Social Fund sets its own agenda for families. One family gets a Community Care Grant from social services - tells the neighbours and others come down to social services. It's an inappropriate referral. Why should they have to go to a social worker to help them get a Community Care grant? (University, Group Two).

One Hallam University student said he would definitely not be happy about advising users on Community Care grants, but as fieldwork findings in other chapters show, there seemed to be confusion and conflict about attitudes and actions because of the desperate need of some users.

Some students felt there was a 'moral panic' by some social services and probation departments, in that they had further limited any cash help they could give users because of a fear of being overwhelmed. The field observations support this view (see Chapters 2 and 6).

Placement supervisors and practice teachers

Students agreed that attitudes of placement supervisors and social workers were extremely variable, but made a crucial difference as to how issues of social work and poverty were handled in practice.

Pete: It depends on the placement whether poverty is part of the job. If your practice teacher doesn't see it as part of your job, how can you?

Avril: My supervisor says, 'You enjoy doing that, so you do it' (welfare rights). But I feel one person is being lumped with it because no-one else knows, especially the younger ones (University, Group Two).

Students from the Hallam University had similar views, but were more critical of supervisors who had deserving/undeserving attitudes towards the poor.

Interviewer: What about practice placements? What sort of attitudes do you think they had towards poverty? Don't necessarily link poverty and welfare rights they might have one attitude toward poverty and one attitude toward welfare rights. Were there different attitudes or were they mixed?

Fran : In South Yorkshire probation there were two probation officers, they started to bring out bulletins on poverty. Now it's early days yet ...but they're appointed full time to look into the issue of poverty, I don't know how that's going to go but at least they've made a start on at least acknowledging that it is an important issue.

Jean: But then last year my practice teacher in social services, I'd better not identify her in any way, said 'Well I think there are two sorts of people, 'the needy and the greedy'...she's quite senior.

Mark: My practice teacher on my first placement was the sort of 'Daily Express blame the victim' and that's the way her social work was. I mean 'somebody else can survive on thirty pounds a week why can't this one - she's smoking too much a week...'

Julie: There's loads of them in social services

Marie: It's going to be really varied isn't it because either you've had good practice teachers who are quite political in social work practice like Bill Smith at the mental health project - that looks very hard at the issue of poverty and everything else. My last placement, I was with a very good practice teacher ...you can draw a short straw with people. I mean I've heard of a woman who was on a course and her practice teacher was sort of saying 'the Social Fund will stop all these young girls wanting to leave home and get pregnant' (Hallam University, Group One).

These sort of comments support theoretical approaches to need that suggest that while social work students may adopt a material or psychological approach to social need, social workers adopt a moral ideology to reduce their own tension and to divide up scarce resources (Smith and Harris 1979).

Martin

Some students felt compromised in their placements because their attitudes and actions to poverty and social work were different from the agency in which they were placed. Martin faced the moral and emotional dilemmas that other students have discussed, by being consistent in his attitudes and actions, which may have been appreciated by the user concerned, but was not by his superiors.

> Martin: I think there is a correlation between certain type of offending and poverty, shop-lifting for example,... some of them perhaps do it for greed but I think the majority of the people who shop-lift they do it out of need, people whose giro hasn't arrived and they've gone to the DSS and they've been fobbed off. I had a man who had not had benefits for four weeks before he actually came to see me, and when I rang up the DSS office and spoke to somebody there he said 'Well tell him to go and eat out of dustbins, people like that are quite used to eating out of dustbins' and I said 'Give me your name', and he wouldn't give me his name and I wanted to hit him you know. It wasn't a professional thing between us anymore, it was a very personal thing and I wanted to just hit this guy and I marched this man down to the office (DSS) and I said I spoke to this guy ...they sort of calmed me down and all the rest of it and got the manager. Course he couldn't produce a person, I had no name and nobody would own up to having said that and I sat with the manager, and said 'Well we're not leaving this office until I get some money it's as simple as that'. And they gave him some money. But he hadn't had any money because he'd been going down every day and he'd been fobbed off until he came to me. In fact my senior wasn't too happy with the course of action I took. I'd marched out of the building with a man down there, sat ourselves down and said 'Right that's it'. I mean I carried on just as much as he was carrying on... you don't go and tell somebody to go and eat out of a dustbin.
>
> Interviewer: What would your senior have liked you to have done?

> Martin: Well, he's actually written to the manager and complained and taken it up with the regional office or somebody like that and not made it into a personal issue. But at that stage I couldn't do anything else - I was so shocked by the guy on the other end of the phone who said, 'Well go tell him to go and eat out of dustbins'. I mean it's true, I live in Leeds and it's a big city and you do see people wandering around eating out of dustbins. It's terrible when people have to get to that. And unfortunately, some social workers I think perhaps are less crusading, perhaps we need to be more crusading in fighting poverty (Hallam University, Group Two)

It is relevant to note that Martin and the user concerned were Afro-Caribbean. It was difficult to separate out Martin's anger concerning the prejudiced comment about poor people, from any feelings that he may have had that he, and his voice is noticeably Afro-Caribbean on the tape, and/or the user were being discriminated against in terms of race. Certainly his actions are different from his supervisor's expectations. He tells the user what DSS have said on the phone, he marches to DSS with the man involved and not only makes it clear to DSS what his complaint is, but also succeeds in securing financial help for the user concerned. Most probation officers would see this way of working as too personal and controversial. However it is likely to be empowering for the black user concerned to observe a black social worker standing up to a prejudiced individual in a government organisation and winning.

Students' views on the future relationship between social work and poverty

All students felt pessimistic about how social workers were going to cope with the financial difficulties of users in the future.

> Gina: I think it's just going to increase the frustration...there's going to be families at rock bottom. It's going to be those very ones that can't get help, and how we're going to handle that.
>
> Interviewer: What's going to have to go, if you're spending more time on dealing with charities...?
>
> Gina: Quite honestly the mind boggles as to what else can actually go, because in some authorities they've already got really high priority cases stacked, so what else can go is the question, not what else will

go. I think the situation is ridiculous, you've got vacancy rates in some London boroughs of about 30 per cent and they just can't recruit workers (University - Group One).

Some had ideas about how social workers could deal with poverty more effectively:

> Gareth: I want to and I've already tried to move towards a more community approach and away from traditional casework...in seeking to tackle poverty because it can't be tackled as an individual and it can't be individualised. I'd see all this leading to me wanting to do less and less of casework and more and more community type work.

> John: I think the long-term future of social work is pretty bleak but I think that the only thing that can happen now is, there's got be some change within social work - the way it operates and the type of work it does. I'm unsure about long-term what goals it would have but I think there are short-term things to be got from it - working away from individualising things that present, to working with people, empowering people...working more with the groups within the community away from the other professionalising influences. But I don't think that's going to happen because as we can see now, social work's statutory and legal powers are going to be increased. We're going to be pulled further and further down that line (Hallam University - Group Two).

Malcolm felt that social workers would not want to be involved with poverty issues:

> Malcolm: I think social work is going to distance itself further from work with money, work with finances. The Social Fund... has made social work departments look closely at how they operate around that ... I think that's meant that social workers have tightened up how they spend money and I can see further constrictions on uses of money within social work (Hallam University - Group One).

Overseas studies

Studies from South Africa and India emphasise that social workers can work with the poor in their communities. Social work students from the University of Witwatersrand were sent on internships to parts of the country where there was extreme rural poverty. They became aware of the stark realities of rural poverty and learnt that trained social workers cannot assume they have the skills to work in any community (Taback and Triegaardt 1992). The Indian study found that communication and interpersonal skills are as important for professionals working in poor communities as the technical content of what they impart (Rustomfram 1991).

It appears that there is no consensus on what students know and need to know in relation to poverty. Schwartz and Robinson's (1991) survey of 119 undergraduate social work students from a mid western US university rated structural explanations of poverty as most important and personal deficiencies of the poor as least important. Problematic areas for the social work curriculum were fatalistic interpretations of poverty and an increasingly external locus of control by the students in relation to poverty issues. However a quantitative study of 137 New York Masters in Social Work students in 1993 found that while social work students' attitudes to the nature of poverty as a structural problem was reinforced, they had severe misconceptions about the economic situation of the poor and did not perceive the poor as being anywhere near as financially deprived as they were in actuality. Even more disappointing were findings from Guttmann and Cohen (1992) in Israel. They found that survey information from 133 students on their perceptions and attitudes towards poverty in five undergraduate social work programmes revealed a surprising lack of difference from the control group of 166 students in programmes unrelated to social work.

A poverty awareness programme

Many of the students in the group discussions in Sheffield said this was the first time that they had discussed the relationship between poverty and social work. The research raised awareness for the students in the same way that the fieldwork findings did for some social workers. Building on these discussions would be the foundation for a poverty awareness course.

The initial and important part of such a course would be to use the individual's personal and professional experiences of poverty to examine their own attitudes. The success of a poverty awareness programme, as with race awareness programmes, would very much depend on the interactions of individuals, including the tutors within the learning group.

Phase one

The programme could consist of three separate learning phases, phase one, two and three. Phase one would be to explore the individual's experience of poverty and is intended to prevent individuals feeling 'blocked' by their own experiences and able to move on, enthusiastic and motivated to phases two and three The group would have to feel at ease with one another before the first part of the programme took place. A deep approach to learning would be developed which could be carried through the programme. Entwistle (1987, p.1) defines a deep approach as:

> Intention to understand, vigorous interaction with content, relate new ideas to previous knowledge, relate concepts to everyday experience, relate evidence to conclusions, examine the logic of the argument.

In phase one individuals would be encouraged to choose a positive commitment concerning poverty which they would discuss with a partner in the group. They would report to that partner at the end of phase three of the programme. Commitments could be big or small, academic or practical. They could involve activities such as: joining the local CPAG group, writing an essay or report on an area of poverty that is work or college related, or conducting a benefits check with all of the social service users with whom the individual comes into contact in their work situation. It might mean working with a user who has chronic financial problems to help him/her become more financially independent and more confident in negotiating with organisations such as fuel companies or debt agencies.

The aim of this phase would be to *challenge* notions of poverty which:

- make distinctions between deserving and undeserving poor,
- see social workers as controlling those in poverty,
- do not contest the gendered or intra household nature of poverty,
- are not aware of the conflicting nature of social workers' attitudes and actions,
- do not integrate the institutional and political aspects of social work into the individual's thinking on poverty.

Phase two

Phase two sessions would aim to integrate theoretical teaching on poverty, and social work with issues that have arisen at work or on placement. Individuals would also be developing personal awareness on poverty and understanding the relationship between poverty and social work. Case studies similar to those used in race awareness training could show how students might deal with an institution or bureaucracy that has no anti-poverty policies or whose policies are not effective in the workplace. These are sessions where the individual is the active participant and the group leader is using questions or case studies to

extend the discussion or to challenge beliefs.
It would establish:

- a definition of poverty and social work,
- the relationship between poverty and social work historically and in the current social and political climate,
- how and in what ways social workers can aid poor social service users,
- what philosophical and ideological perspectives support the use of practical aid to poor people.

Phase Three

Phase three may require more than one external tutor with expertise in presenting welfare rights and tax benefits to students in an accessible and understandable style. It would cover all aspects of welfare rights and tax benefits for people on a low income but in a form that would give students confidence. It could include:

- administering basic benefits checks,
- administration and policy guidelines regarding the Social Fund
- updating on changes to policy and legislation - for example the tax credit system in the 1998 Budget for families with children and disabled people
- the procedures at DSS tribunals - acting as an advocate
- Using key texts for reference on welfare benefits and tax benefits for low income families

In all phases, there should be a clear conception of the subject being studied and its relevance to social work, the benefits of the teaching method employed, and a comprehensive assessment, by participants of what they have learned.

Conclusions

The fieldwork findings from this chapter suggest that students are truly concerned and knowledgeable about the relationship between poverty and social work. Recommendations that would aid social work students in dealing with the sensitive and difficult issues of financial deprivation include:

- When faced with allocating small amounts of money to large numbers of people, it appears that a rationing system is bound to emerge. Advising social service users of their benefit rights, so giving users a feeling of entitlement rather than deprivation and stigma may be a more effective policy for social work students and social workers. Only one out of forty nine students involved in the group discussions conducted basic benefits checks with users. Other students mentioned welfare rights or community work as a strategy to help users with financial difficulties. The reality of working or being on placement in a social services department seems in general removed from the principal stand of those such as Fimister (1986) and Stewart (ed. 1989, p.24):

> We have established the extent to which social work tasks concern people who are poor, homeless, ill housed or jobless. Whatever the setting, client group, or work method, these problems seem bound to increase in prominence within social work practice. We have argued that credibility with clients will be enhanced if social workers engage these problems, however bleak the prospects for significant material change. We have also argued that social work needs to adopt a rights approach. This is not because there are well established and defined rights to a basic minimum income, to a decent home or to a job, but rather because it can counter demoralisation and dependency by the assertion of dignity, human worth and citizenship.

- The evidence presented here from overseas supports the need for further study and discussion on social work courses regarding issues of poverty and inequality. There is also a history of research in this country which advocates more specific content in social work courses concerning financial deprivation (Donnison 1955, MacGrail 1983, Noble and Stewart 1987, Davies and Wright 1989, Davies, Grimwood and Stewart 1987, Parsloe 1990).

- The use of qualitative data in this study has tended to reinforce the findings of some quantitative studies which stress the importance of this part of the social work syllabus. More importantly qualitative research has highlighted the complex emotional, intellectual and moral issues that students have to cope with outside the academic environment. A poverty awareness programme would allow students to contribute and learn from each other and sort out their personal and political stand on poverty while in training. Their own attitudes and actions may thus be more consistent when they commence their professional work.

6 Social workers' attitudes and actions in relation to poor social service users

This chapter is concerned with understanding social workers' attitudes and actions in relation to the poverty of social service users. The findings are based on two participant observation studies - nine months with the Silverton social work team and five months with the City team. The first part of the chapter introduces a social psychological and social constructionist model to understand the interactions in the fieldwork. The second part of the chapter reviews previous research findings and compares them with this study. The third part of the chapter analyses the research findings in three different areas concerned with the relationship between social work and poverty - section 17 money, 'deserving' and 'undeserving' poor; and finally welfare benefits. A comparatively small number of fieldwork examples are given and analysed which are representative of a much greater number. After thirteen months field observation the amount of data that could have been included was enormous.

The majority of social workers and social service users interviewed and observed in the Silverton area were white, female and from working class backgrounds. Social workers in the Silverton team were local to the area and thus they had in one sense more rapport with local users, although there was also more opportunity for utilising local knowledge of individuals which did not come through official channels.

City team had a wider mix of clients in terms of race and gender but few who were middle class. The social workers in the City team were mostly university educated and generally 'progressive' in their attitudes and outlooks. There were no black social workers employed with either team during the field observation period, although one of the female social work students in City team was black.

Social workers' attitudes and actions

> Carol: What I found quite interesting was that you expected to find that peoples' attitudes would relate to their own background and I would have expected that as well. But what was I think *really* interesting is the fact that attitudes and actions don't marry up. If you come up with a piece of research and the findings are that the attitudes of social workers don't bear any relation to what *then* happens on the ground roots. The fact you related that to policy makers, I think that's quite important (Silverton social worker, discussing a feedback paper on the research).

Social workers' attitudes to poverty are influenced by: personal factors such as schooling and professional training, present and past family situations, interactions with social service users, the social services hierarchy, and team members; and institutional factors such as the policies and bureaucracies of the social services department and local and central government departments (Parsloe 1978, Satyamurti 1981, Becker 1987). If these attitudes have no direct effect on social workers' practice, not much can be said about what social workers *do* in relation to poverty or what they could do differently - nor whether poverty awareness programmes would be effective. Such attitudes and actions cannot be considered without examining the wider context in which social workers operate, understanding the pressure that is above or around social workers that they may pass on to users. Ethnography is considered a qualitative method which understands rather than counts or proscribes. Therefore this chapter will present the fieldwork findings from an individual interactive perspective, rather than the social, structural perspective explored in Chapter 2.

Consistency between attitudes and actions is a common problem for every individual, and social workers are not different. It is often expected that people in professional caring roles have superior moral standards. This is unrealistic. The chapter does not intend to judge individual social workers by pointing out contradictions in their attitudes and actions, but to understand how these contradictions came about. A further development from the theoretical positions explored and the fieldwork findings examined, is to ask to what extent are attitudes discrete and different entities from actions.

Theoretical models for understanding attitudes and actions

It would be simplistic to assume social workers have an all encompassing attitude to poverty which can be assessed by their practice with poor people, nor can an attitude be measured merely by observing consistencies in behaviour. Cook and Selltiz (1964, p.64) define attitude as:

> an underlying disposition which enters, *along with other influences*, into the determination of a variety of behaviours toward an object or class of objects, including statements of beliefs and feelings about the object and approach-avoidance actions with respect to it.

The interesting question from this definition is what *are* the other influences that determine behaviour and how do attitudes interact with them?

Dollard (1949, p.624) suggests a high degree of consistency between words and acts is essential,

> It enables men to participate in organised social life with good confidence that others will do what they say they will do, will be where they say they will be. Valid prediction of behaviour is not a mere luxury of morality, but a vital social necessity. Every man is under compulsion to keep his promises, to make his acts correspond with his verbal expressions. He constantly watches others to see that they do likewise.

Wicker (1973) maintains that we are trained from childhood to expect attitude - behaviour consistency, particularly among public officials. To suggest social workers' attitudes and actions are not as consistent as one would expect, is to cross a strong moral boundary. Furthermore as Fishbein (1967) suggests, if the behaviour is public rather than private, beliefs about the consequences of actions will be more marked.

Social psychological theories

Psychological research on the relationship between attitudes and behaviour has centred around two related theories.

Theory of reasoned action
The first 'theory of reasoned action' (Ajzen and Fishbein 1977, 1980, Manstead, Proffit and Smart 1983), suggests that the stronger a persons

intention, the more the person is expected to try and the greater the likelihood that the behaviour will be performed. The determinants of intention are conceived as *attitude towards the behaviour* - a favourable or unfavourable evaluation of the behaviour in question; and *subjective norm* - the perceived social pressure to perform or not to perform the behaviour. Attitude and subjective norm, weighted for their relative importance, are jointly assumed to determine behavioural intention and thus behaviour. There are three conditions attached to this theory. Firstly the measure of intention must correspond to the behavioural criterion. Predicting a specific action of social workers in relation to poor users must be compared with an equally specific intention. Secondly the intention must not have changed in the time between when it was assessed and the time when the behaviour is observed. The accuracy of prediction will usually vary inversely with the time interval between intention and observed behaviour. Thirdly the behaviour under consideration must be under volitional control.

> ...the more that performance of the behaviour is contingent on the presence of appropriate opportunities or on possession of adequate resources (time, money, skills, cooperation of other people, etc), the less the behaviour is under volitional control (Ajzen and Madden 1985, p.455).

Thus the theory of reasoned action which relies on intention as the sole predictor of action will be insufficient whenever control over the behavioural goal is incomplete. Factors which interfere with control over intended behaviour include those internal to the individual - skills, abilities, knowledge and adequate planning; and external ones - time, opportunity, financial resources and dependence of the behaviour on the co-operation of other people.

Control over intended behaviour is a key issue in the understanding of social workers' and students' attitudes and actions towards those in poverty. Many social workers and students (see Chapters 2 and 5) felt powerless to help and advise poor social service users because of lack of time, knowledge and financial resources, despite there being no lack of appropriate opportunities.

Theory of planned behaviour

The second theoretical position proposes a 'theory of planned behaviour' which extends the theory of reasoned action by including the concept of behavioural control. It suggests that among the beliefs that ultimately determine intention and action is a set that deals with the presence or absence of resources and opportunities. The more resources and opportunities individuals think they possess and the fewer obstacles they anticipate, the greater should be their perceived control over behaviour (Schifter and Ajzen 1985, Bagozzi 1992, Mcbroom and Reed 1992). Bandura and his associates (cited in Tesser 1995) note that people's behaviour is strongly influenced by their confidence in their ability to perform the behaviour.

Karen - Silverton social work team

Karen had little confidence in her ability and knowledge of welfare rights issues and her behaviour towards users with financial problems reflected this lack of confidence. She felt the subject area was too complex and during the nine months field observation I did not observe her conducting any basic benefits checks or giving welfare rights advice to users in the waiting room or out on visits. Karen also perceived herself as having little power or control in the allocation of social security monies.

> Karen: I mean y'know very well before you sort of pick the phone up, it's going to be a no go anyway. It's just an exercise isn't it?... go through the motions and it's so time consuming, as well and at the end of the day, he's not going to get anything is he?

When Brian Lunt the local welfare rights officer and his assistant came to talk to the team about fuel debts, her body posture and facial expression suggested that she had little interest. On the other hand, the amount of information Brian Lunt gave at the meeting, and the level of complexity and the speed at which the lecture on fuel debts was delivered was such that even those social workers who were motivated to tackle welfare rights issues found the session difficult to follow. It seems likely that Karen felt 'de-skilled' after the session, as she complained it was 'above her'.

Having observed this attempt by the team leader to introduce more welfare rights knowledge into the team, the feedback papers suggested that information on welfare rights could be introduced using a problem solving approach (see Appendix 3). This could involve team members bringing poverty or welfare rights problems to a forum for discussion where the welfare rights officer acts as an adviser.

Bandura et al (1980) also suggest that people who believe they have neither the resources nor the opportunities to perform a certain behaviour are unlikely to form strong behavioural intentions to engage in it, even if they hold favourable attitudes towards the behaviour and believe that important others would approve of their performing the behaviour. Most members of the City social work team and some members of the Silverton team had positive attitudes towards the role of welfare rights in social work, but felt overwhelmed by casework and statutory duties and therefore were frustrated in their actions, despite their attitudes.

Poverty awareness

The theoretical concepts described have implications for the training of social workers and students in relation to poverty issues. In terms of a poverty awareness programme for example, the concept of perceived control, confidence, resources and opportunities would have to be addressed in relation to the busy working environment of social workers. So would subjective norms - the influence of family and friends and individuals in the work environment, both in the past and present. Training exercises which ask students to assess influences on their behaviour, and empower individuals in terms of their confidence and abilities to make a positive impact regarding poverty issues in the workplace, may be more important initially than the more objective teaching of welfare rights.

A critique of the social psychological perspective

The psychological model of planned behaviour (see Figure 6.1), will be employed where appropriate in this chapter because it can highlight the complexities and interactions observed in the fieldwork setting. This model emphasises more strongly the effect of *perceived* control on behaviour rather than actual control (Norman and Smith, 1995).

A strong effect of perceived behavioural control is expected under only two conditions. Firstly that the behaviour being predicted must not be under complete volitional control. Social workers', students' and users' actions are undoubtedly influenced by a number of factors outside their own control. Secondly the perceptions of behavioural control must accurately reflect actual control in the situation with some degree of accuracy. For example are Karen's comments about welfare rights being a waste of time fair? Is she as powerless as she thinks? Unrealistic perceived behavioural control could be assessed and discussed in training programmes on poverty awareness, for example - how much time will management actually allow for welfare rights training?. However as Ajzen and Madden (1986, p.460) note:

> ...the idea that both intention and control are necessary for performance of a behaviour ...suggests an interaction effect, such that the effect of intention on behaviour depends on perceived behavioural control.

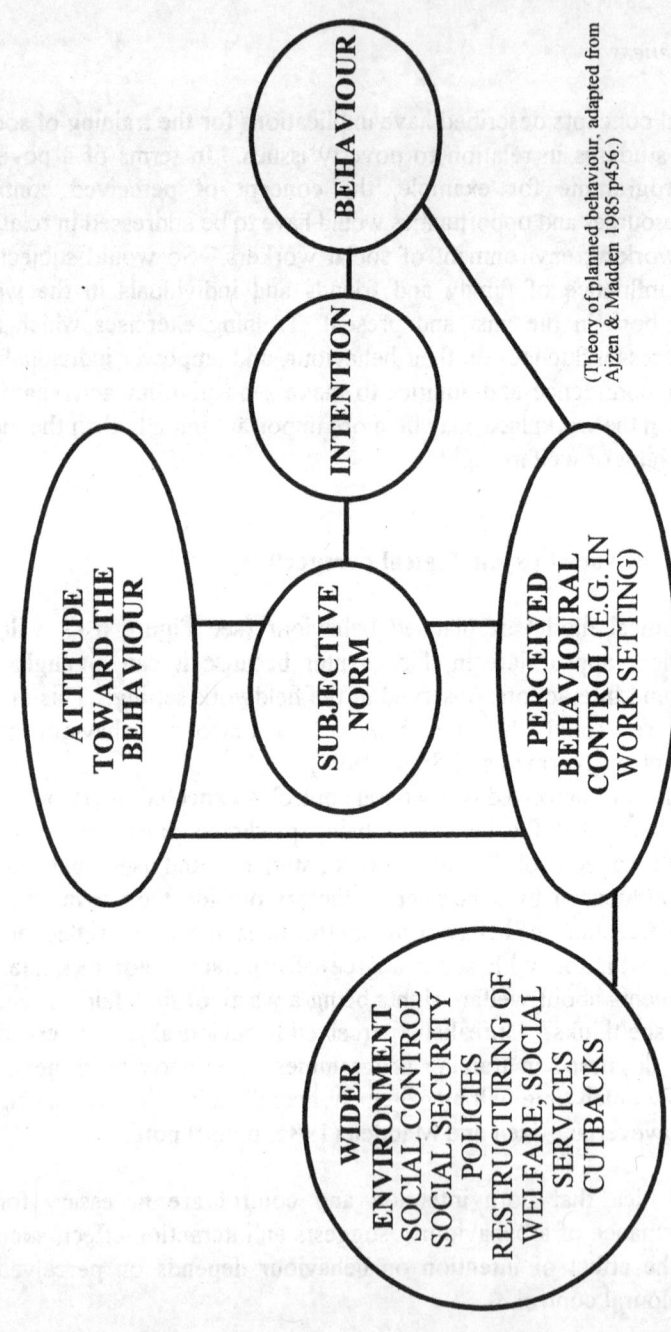

(Theory of planned behaviour, adapted from Ajzen & Madden 1985 p456.)

Figure 6.1 A social/psychological view of the relationship between attitudes and actions

Interaction in the fieldwork setting is often complex and ambiguous and cannot always be tested in a controlled experimental setting in the way that these psychological concepts appear to require. For example the theory of reasoned action has as one of its three conditions that intention must not have changed in the time between when it was assessed and the time when the behaviour was observed, and that accuracy of prediction will usually vary inversely with the time interval between intention and observed behaviour. This condition appears more relevant to experimental situations than observed reality in a social services department. There were occasions when social workers would discuss their intentions immediately prior to acting upon them but there were other occasions when a social worker would voice an intention in a team meeting - for example, to organise a meeting on welfare rights - and it would be some weeks later before that intention was acted upon.

Social construction

A further theoretical framework that highlights the difficulties of defining set attitudes and actions in relation to poverty is that of the social constructionists (Edwards and Potter 1992). They are concerned with how accounts and actions construct reality and use participant observation data to produce accounts of motivation in naturally occurring situations - in this case social work practice.

Their theoretical framework differs from psychological concepts explored because they would not assume a fixed or objective reality where 'real' attitudes exist. In relation to the fieldwork a perspective which examines behaviour and includes all attitudes and actions can provide insight into why social workers' attitudes and actions were not always consistent. Social constructionists would argue that social workers would account for their social work practice differently on different occasions depending on the purpose of the discussion and to whom they were talking. Both social/psychological and social constructionist theories can provide a useful understanding of social workers' attitudes and actions in the fieldwork setting.

Previous research on social workers' attitudes to poverty

> ...few social workers have any developed insight into how their ideologies and perceptions of poverty affect their daily practice with poor people ...on an individual level attitudes are not always consistent, nor are they consistently supportive (Becker 1987, p.243, 247).

The relationship between social workers' attitudes and actions in relation to poverty has been neglected in the literature. Craig and Coxall (1989) list 227 accounts of investigations into the Social Fund. This one aspect of social workers' dealings with poor people is researched in terms of policy issues and attitudes. Of the 44 studies which deal with the relationship between social workers and the Social Fund, not one explores the importance of connections between social workers' attitudes *and actions*.

Parsloe and Stevenson (1978) and Becker (1987) encountered social workers' attitudes to poverty at a particular time and place. A study that *only* researches attitudes fails to understand the complexity of working in a busy social services office. In Becker's 1986 survey of 450 social workers, it was found that the following characteristics were associated with a 'positive' attitude towards the poor:

> Youth (25-40); those with a degree and CQSW; with some experience of claiming benefit; who had decided to become social workers early in their lives or while unemployed; lived in small cities in their childhood and now live in relatively deprived areas; with prior experience of social work related or voluntary work, and who are relatively new to social work practice... They were more likely to view poverty in structural terms, support the Labour party and pressure groups such as CPAG and have strong supportive feelings towards the poor (Becker 1987, p.497).

However even if an individual possessed all of these characteristics, they cannot be assumed to have a 'positive' attitude to the poor. Is it possible to define a 'positive' attitude to poverty in the way Becker (1987) proposes? This research questions the existence of two dimensional 'positive' and 'negative' attitudes to poverty by illustrating the complexity of the interaction of attitudes and actions in the fieldwork.

Fieldwork findings

Vernon, the Silverton team leader

If a 'positive' attitude to poverty can be defined as social workers having the intention to take principled actions (see Figure 6.1) to aid those social service users in poverty, then Vernon the Silverton team leader, demonstrated 'positive' actions and attitudes in refusing to be involved with income maintenance issues. His principled stand was that giving ad hoc material aid was the responsibility of the DSS, and that social workers should not be involved with income maintenance because it undermined a rights approach to poverty.

> Vernon: I think there's a difference between giving welfare advice Beverly, and a specialised system of knowledge I've acquired over the last few years and using that knowledge. There's a difference between that and dealing with someone that everybody else has passed on and we'd better sort them out and it's the second situation I'm talking about...

He had a radicalising effect on other team members and tended to recruit social workers who had similar structural views of the world. He had been the first team leader to pay out Section 1 money to miners' families in the miners' strike. However during the nine months field observation of the team, Vernon's attitudes to alleviating poverty through income maintenance could be characterised by:

> I can't free myself of a sense of generalised resentment when some poor person comes in for food vouchers... I resent *anybody* having to come into this office ... and have to give them financial help (Yes - from other members of the team), not because I would feel these people don't need it, but because it's a symptom of what society does. And at the end of the day every Friday afternoon, we have to give them a small bit of money, which bears no relation at all to where they are in the world or their problems. ...I mean the effectiveness of us as social workers. We're just caught in a symptomatic situation that's very very frustrating, and I often feel quite angry because I mean, people come and say 'I haven't got any money', and 'I haven't got ...' and I'll try and repress that and I'm sure that at times I don't succeed, because it's a generalised anger about what we do as social workers or what we're told we have to do, which is irrelevant within the broader spectrum, or what we were trained for or what we feel.

The actions that resulted from these attitudes included dissuading other social work staff from being involved in community care grants and being reluctant to authorize Section 17 payments unless the money was used as part of on-going preventative casework. Both actions could be said to be consistent with Vernon's attitudes towards social workers not being involved with income maintenance issues. He had also been involved in drafting a social services paper advising social workers not to co-operate with the DSS. From a social service user perspective, Vernon may well have been seen as having a 'negative' attitude to poverty in that he was not prepared to alleviate their financial distress through cash payments if they had not had previous 'casework' contact with a social worker.

Regarding the relationship between attitudes and actions, two further points illustrate its complexity. Firstly social workers' attitudes may change over time, and depend on external factors.

> Vernon: The miners' strike was different...that was more to do with politics and that was a uniform response, but these dribs and drabs...

Secondly 'intense feelings towards the poor' (Becker 1987, p.497) may result in the individual social worker feeling frustrated and angry at how little social work can affect poverty and therefore as in this example, attitudes and actions in relation to income maintenance becoming more 'negative' than a social worker with less intense feelings towards the poor and the role of the government and the DSS. Vernon felt that he had no control over the poverty of most social service users. This perceived lack of control affected his attitudes, intentions and behaviour (see Figure 6.1).

Observation studies

Although questionnaires, focus group discussions and in depth interviews are utilised to understand social workers' attitudes, field observation in this study proved essential to uncover significant interactions between attitudes and actions in relation to poverty issues. Other observation studies have provided useful insights into behaviour rather than attitudes alone. Cooper's observation study of ten DSS offices researched attitudes and actions of DSS staff to claimants both when staff were on duty on the counter and out on visits. Cooper (1985, p.51) found that:

> ...treatment of claimants could vary according to a judgement made about them by officers, on the basis of very little information and a brief acquaintance.

However there is no in depth discussion in the study of how and to what extent attitudes were translated into actions. Cooper appears to assume from his observations that attitudes and actions are consistent where DSS officers act on what they perceive as their professional judgement.

In Pithouse's observation study of two social work teams specialising in child care, he makes the following comments regarding social workers' attitudes to financial issues,

> There is little doubt that the child care workers operate with a clientele who are materially disadvantaged. Yet like workers elsewhere (Parsloe and Stevenson 1978, p.324, Satyamurti 1981, p.168-175) they view their involvement in welfare rights and financial matters as an undignified departure from their preferred style of practice...There is also the view that 'money' sullies the relationship between client and worker. Indeed requests by clients for financial help suggests they have incorrectly grasped the purpose of child care work and are attempting to impose their definition on a service that practitioners intend to manage and control. (Pithouse 1987, p.82)

Although Pithouse's research was based in an area office with two teams who both specialise in child care, it does not include observations of interactions between social workers and users. Nor can it appreciate the significant differences between the two teams observed in this study because they were based in different locations and they were employed by different local authorities.

Satyamurti (1981), Smith (1980) and Pithouse (1987) imply that social workers' attitudes are constantly dynamic and changing, mainly affected by the institution in which they work and their interactions with the hierarchy and colleagues. However a social services department is not a total institution and social workers interact with family, friends and others outside the social services departments. They also have professional autonomy. For example many social workers are professionally committed to the empowerment of users and carers. Such attitudes can cause conflict if they are at variance with a particular aim or practice of the institution.

Parsloe and Stevenson (1978) and Becker (1997) show a 'snapshot' of social workers' attitudes at a particular time and place. Even if these findings are illustrative of social workers' attitudes rather than representative or replicable, the authors tend to assume that responses to poverty issues are transferable to different times, places, organisations and individuals. Their research findings tend to 'fit' with social psychological concepts on attitudes and behaviour which suggest a more static concept of attitude than the sociological perspective described previously.

Figure 6.2 indicates how previous research has understood social workers' attitudes in relation to poverty and how these research studies can be linked to different epistemological roots. As a result of the fieldwork findings, it is suggested that some of social workers' responses to poverty are determined by their environment while other responses to poverty are preformed and

> Becker (1997); Parsloe and Stevenson (1978). The 'snapshot' approach to attitudes of social workers to poverty. Social Workers attitudes to poverty are individual, pre-formed and static.

*
*
*
*
*
*
*
*
*

> **This Research**
> Social Workers' attitudes *and actions* in relation to poverty. Individual attitudes and actions are sometimes influenced by the organisation or interactions with colleagues and sometimes by individual pre-formed attitudes.

*
*
*
*
*
*
*

> Satyamurti (1981), Smith (1980) and Pithouse (1987) suggest the ideologies of social workers are mainly influenced by the organisations in which they work, and the interactions between members of that organisation.

Figure 6.2 The research findings in relation to previous research findings on social workers' attitudes to poverty

relatively unchanging. The findings also suggest that social workers do not always reveal consistent attitudes, intentions or behaviours in relation to poverty issues.

The Child Care Act 1980 Section 1, replaced by Section 17 of the Children Act (1989), allows social workers to give cash help to parents to prevent their children coming into or continuing to be in care. Section 12 in Scotland has a wider brief which does not only include monies for children and families. Actual amounts spent vary between local authorities from £2,000 to over £1 million although this could include expenditure on preventive services such as day care.

Food, food vouchers and primarily direct cash help were the only forms of income maintenance that social workers or team leaders had the power to authorize (see Chapter 1). There was high demand for such monies from social service users who came to the duty desk and social workers in both teams disliked taking turns at duty - covering all the public enquiries that came in on a particular day or half day. Social workers' attitudes to Section 17 money in both teams were generally negative. They felt uncomfortable about being in the position of judging who should and who should not get cash help.

Mrs Grant

Mrs Grant was looking after her two grandchildren aged three and five years. Her daughter was in prison and she was living on £42 a week income support. She had come to social services because probation had sent her - they were helping her with furniture after her daughter's flat had been burgled. Welfare rights had suggested she come to social services when they could not get her child benefit sorted out with DSS - she had not had any child benefit for six weeks since her daughter had gone to prison. She admitted, 'I went to borrow money from a neighbour and she said to come here...It's really the bus fares I can't manage'. Her daughter lived some distance from her, so it was two buses each way to the local school. What did the social worker do? Firstly he checked out her story. Secondly he said social services did not have any money. He then said abruptly without explanation, 'Well we could take the children into care'. Mrs Grant looked horrified and became quite aggressive about whether there was a scheme to provide toys at the office. Keith went to check with the receptionist. He also offered to ring DSS to sort out her child benefit but she said welfare rights was already doing this. She chatted to me while he was gone.

> Mrs Grant: I was really dreading coming here.
>
> Interviewer: Is it as bad as you thought?

Mrs Grant: Don't know - what *he* said was.

Interviewer: You mean about going into care?

Mrs Grant: Yes.

I explained it was a procedure so that social services could pay her as a foster mother. It did not mean she was a 'bad' grandmother. She seemed reassured but said, 'No I wouldn't want to do it'.

Later Keith admitted that the statement about the children going into care was, 'partly as a deterrent to stop people keep coming back for money'. I had assumed he was thinking he could apply for social services to take responsibility for the children on paper and then apply to the fostering panel for the grandmother to become the foster mother. However he had asked no further questions of Mrs Grant regarding taking the children into care - for example how long was her daughter likely to be in prison. (I had recently read a memo he had written to the divisional officer arguing strongly for a grandmother who was a client of his to be put forward to the fostering panel as a foster parent for her two grandchildren. The regular Section 17 money this grandmother had been receiving from the department had been withdrawn.)

Mrs Grant did receive £5 from Section 17 money though I suspect Keith would have preferred to give her nothing but felt constrained by the observation. Although Mrs Grant might not come back to social services as she seemed genuinely frightened, she could quite easily tell friends and neighbours that she had received £5, so the deterrent effect of threatening to take the children into care would be lost.

City team budgets

Later that day Keith told me he had only got £15 left to spend on duty cases. Bernard, the team leader had told him that the limit was £30 per day as the social services budget was overspent after the first six months of the year. Another social worker had spent £10 not knowing about the £30 limit, and Mrs Grant had £5. We were discussing a woman with twins who had rung him up to say DSS had not sent her milk tokens. He was worried she was going to come in and ask for money, 'If you try to spend more on duty, admin would stop you.'

Maria, the administrative officer confirmed this when she said, 'I'm not supposed to keep a tally in the office but I do.' She would also be checking that none of the four teams she was responsible for spent over £30 per month per family, another recent financial cutback in terms of Section 17 monies. I asked her, 'Do teams go over their limit?' and she responded very definitely, 'Yes!'

Keith had management pressure to keep within a financial budget. The administrative officer was acting as the department's gatekeeper. As well as not wanting to be a second string DSS officer - and his actions concerning income maintenance put him in this category - he also wanted to be seen as a 'good' social worker.

The social psychological model

From both psychological and sociological perspectives, it is not surprising that Keith's actions were congruent with his attitudes. In terms of Ajzen and Madden's model, Keith perceives behavioural control in the work setting - a limit on Section 17 payments monitored by the team leader and the administrative officer - affecting his attitude towards users with financial difficulties. Subjective norms of some colleagues and other staff in the workplace appear to support the notion that income maintenance is not the job of social workers, should be sorted out by DSS and is an inconvenience to social work and administrative staff. Some staff also made the distinction between 'deserving' (mostly people who did not come to social services at all) and 'undeserving' (those people who knew about Section 17 money and were able to weave a credible 'hard luck' story). Although Keith's own attitudes may not appear to make such clear distinctions, according to Ajzen and Madden's model he would be affected by the subjective norms of others. Even if Keith would generally feel more sympathetic to people in poverty, he experiences feelings of powerlessness, not only because of the perceived controls and subjective norms in the work setting but because of formal policies in the wider environment which have caused cutbacks in local authorities' funding and a more restrictive system for those claiming benefits.

The social constructionist model

From a social constructionist perspective both attitudes and actions are forms of behaviour and cannot easily be separated into discrete units. Individuals thus construct their behaviour which includes attitudes in order to accomplish social actions (Edwards and Potter 1992). Keith's comments on a number of occasions were cynical about people coming to social services for money. He seemed to see the process as some sort of game with them 'trying it on' and him 'turning them off,

> The regulars come in after 3.30 on Friday when social security is closed. They know they can get Section 17 payments for the weekend. We're caught.

This process implies different attitudes and actions for the different 'players in the game' and has different outcomes according to social constructionist theory for Keith, Mrs Grant, Maria and other receptionists at social services - however no *one* account of the process is the 'true' account.

> The psychologist's (or sociologist's) privileged position of being able to define, over the heads of participants, the true nature of events has proved a powerful one in experimental studies, but it is a position that can also be illusory (there is no single, definitive version of everyday events), and risks losing sight of what is real for participants themselves. It focuses attention on objective truth and error, and underestimates the constructive, occasioned and rhetorically designed nature of how events are ordinarily described (Edwards and Potter 1992, p.5).

'What really happened' in this observed event will differ according to the participant, although Mrs Grant's version of events has no power or authority attached to it.

Team policies on Section 17 monies

The Administrative officer in controlling financial resources in relation to Section 17 money is in a powerful position. It is likely that in the same way that social workers exercise discretion when doling out money to those who have come for financial help, she exercises discretion about which social workers she favours and gives money to. This could be seen to be 'policy making on the hoof.' It is created as it is implemented. A new team leader or social worker joins the team, a well established one leaves, a new admin officer commences work, one who 'knows the ropes' leaves, receptionists change. Policy on Section 17 payments will drift according to who is exercising what discretion, and the power of the individual user in constructing their version of events.

The attitudes and actions of the team leader with regard to income maintenance may be extremely important until of course he or she leaves and the next team leader has a different management policy.

City team

In the City social work team, social workers could 'pp' their team leader's signature on the Section 17 forms. They used their discretion about who should and should not get cash, subject to the cash limits that had been imposed on them by higher management. City team seemed quite proud that although some teams had been giving some families £30 a week and the new guide-lines were £30 a month, 'We try to keep it down to £30 per family every 3 months'. The impression they were giving was that they were an efficient team who managed their budget well.

Silverton team

In the Silverton team, Vernon, the team leader was unlikely to sign the Section 17 forms unless they were part of ongoing work with the family. His attitudes and actions initially appeared central to the way the team operated in relation to income maintenance. However Vernon's attitudes and actions were only a 'subjective norm' for the rest of the team in the formal setting of team meetings. Out of the office social workers often provided cash from their own pockets, either as a gift or a loan, if they thought an individual or family were 'deserving'. Karen told me that she would often give cash or food to mothers with young children because she could identify with their plight, having been in a similar situation with four children herself. I observed Tina receiving the return of a loan of £5. When I questioned whether this was a covert activity, she replied that on the contrary, most social workers in the team were involved in this form of private income maintenance. Although social workers in the team appeared to take a principled stand against income maintenance in team meetings, in practice their actions were contradictory. So despite not having the same access to 'official' forms of income maintenance that City social workers had, Silverton social workers would also feel pressure to respond personally to the financial needs of social service users.

Tight management and administrative controls of limited financial resources implies that the behaviour of the two social work teams can be predicted in relation to giving out Section 17 monies. Subjective norms in the City team suggest that limiting and controlling cash paid out to social service users makes them efficient managers as compared to other teams. The Silverton team on the other hand, have norms that suggest Section 17 money is only paid out for on-going casework and not for income maintenance. The social workers feel they have little power to alter administrative rules or financial restrictions, although in fact another social work team in the City authority deliberately overspent their Section 17 budget in order to show the extent of financial need in their area.

Miss Lerner and Section 17 monies

The receptionist came in to say that Miss Lerner was in reception. She had nothing on her file but had come in, 'cos she hasn't got any money and thought you could give her some.' Miss Lerner was separated with a child aged two. She usually borrowed from her mother on Friday and paid her back on Monday. This week her mother did not want to lend her any money and said she 'ought to manage on her own by now'. Jane, one of the City Team's social workers, went to see her on duty and came back to the office to confer. She said to Bernard, the team leader, 'help me make a decision I'm tired....What she's actually asking is to borrow it. I said we don't do that'. Miss Lerner was not aware of and was not informed of the Social Fund loan system but she had got milk tokens from the DSS. The team leader asked about practical help through her health visitor. Miss Lerner had said, 'I wouldn't dare ask, she thinks I cope so well.' Bernard said Miss Lerner could not have Section 17 money and Jane went back to tell her.

> Jane: If you'd been battering your children or something we could help, but not in this case.
>
> Miss Lerner: Well I'm not that bad.

Miss Lerner had not learnt to 'play the game' in admitting that she had a relative that might be prepared to help her if social services could not. 'There goes one dissatisfied customer' sighed Jane. She discussed the irony of not being able to help people *unless* they reach crisis with their children. She rang the health visitor as Bernard had suggested but she could not help with Miss Lerner's finances. I was aware that Miss Lerner might not have wanted Jane to phone the health visitor. Not only had she gone away with no money for the weekend, her health visitor was likely to review her impression of Miss Lerner as someone who could cope. Miss Lerner was not 'deserving enough' or did not put her case strongly enough for her to be given Section 17 money. The social worker's attitude to Section 17 payments was not the same as the policies of the department in which she worked. Jane felt the tension between her attitudes, subjective norms, perceived behavioural control, intentions and actual behaviour.

A moral ideology of need

Ideology of need can be defined as:

> ...systems of ideas in terms of which social work professionals make

sense of their everyday practice and of the administrative structure in which this occurs (Smith and Harris 1979, p.57).

Thus Jane's response to financial need contained certain moral ideas. Firstly it was assumed that because Miss Lerner's mother had helped her in the past, she would do so this time, despite Miss Lerner explaining that her mother had said she would not. Social Services tended to assume that local relatives could financially support the social service user and would be willing to do so. In this sense Miss Lerner is not *really* 'deserving'. Secondly she is not deserving enough because she has not an on-going casework relationship with a social worker, and thirdly Miss Lerner has not, it seems, maltreated her child in any way. If there was no moral ideology attached to giving out Section 17 money, it would be allocated on first come, first served basis.

Policy implications - income maintenance

There are many other examples from the fieldwork which show that giving or not giving direct financial aid is the most common way in which social workers deal with the poverty of social service users. The example quoted is illustrative of many more where the user either gets no money at all or a small amount. Even on a rationing/rule book or a 'first come, first served' system, there would under the present system of central and local government budgeting, not be sufficient resources to help all those in financial need. Government legislation and policy seems to indicate the financial role of the social worker is likely to become a greater part of the social work task in the future in a number of different ways:

- the social worker as community care purchaser rather than provider,
- the social worker administering community care charging policies,'
- the social worker as organiser of direct payments for users and carers,
- the social worker advising on benefits to maximise income,
- the social worker having to make direct cash payments due to low benefit entitlement.

How can social workers and others - professionals and claimants/clients be better prepared for this? Firstly if the link between cash and care is to be effective, it must be based on some commonly accepted minimum income for all. Secondly an ombudsman who safeguards citizen's rights regarding cash and caring decisions would probably be more relevant than the tribunal system for social security questions. Social services departments who are necessarily involved in financial dealings with users and carers should be willing to have their decisions subject to scrutiny.

Research findings - 'deserving' and 'undeserving' poor

Attitudes and actions which distinguished between 'deserving' and 'undeserving' poor appeared more marked in the Silverton team than the City team. The length of time spent with Silverton (nine months) as compared to City team (five months) could mean that Silverton social workers were more relaxed in my presence and consequently more open in what they were saying and doing. City team seemed more aware than the Silverton team that they were being studied and therefore may have been careful of what they said and did.

The social constructionist model

Dianne, one of the most experienced social workers in the City team was talking to one of the home help organizers in the office in my presence.

> Home help organiser: She's applying for a third grant, she's already had two, plus she's on full attendance allowance and she lives alone. She gets a disability pension and mobility allowance.
>
> Dianne: Well I hope you said 'good luck' to her.
>
> Home help organiser: Well I don't know what she spends it on - it was a long 'phone call but she gets that through disability.

Discourse analysis and social constructionist would suggest that in saying things, people perform social actions. The home help organizer was not from the City team and would not be aware of the participant observation study or its purpose. Dianne as a member of the social work team was aware of my interest in their conversation and how I might think that she was colluding with the Home help organizer in agreeing that the user concerned was undeserving of the benefits she received. In more 'natural' circumstances without my presence, Dianne might have decided to smile and agree, not wanting to offend a colleague while still being aware of her own different point of view. On field observation visits with Dianne, she appeared particularly sensitive to money issues and it would seem unlikely that she would have agreed with the Home help organizer that a social service user was receiving too much benefit without a careful analysis of the facts.

This fieldwork example can be used as an illustration of the constructionist' perspective that social interaction is subjectively situated and will vary, depending on time, place, individuals present and environment. So Dianne's attitude in terms of 'deserving' and 'undeserving' poor cannot be measured as an objective entity but will depend on the specific context of the situated action for which it is constructed (Edwards and Potter 1992).

The social/psychological model

In terms of the social/psychological model however Dianne's comments to the Home help organiser could be explained in terms of the subjective norm with which the home help organizer wished Dianne to agree. This was not attractive to Dianne in terms of other colleagues' subjective norms, her own attitude and non stigmatising social work policies in the workplace towards social service users. The perceived behavioural control in this situation rested with Dianne as a senior social worker especially as the home help organizer was not from her team. Dianne's attitude, intention and behaviour were straightforward and consistent in not agreeing with the comments made and then changing the subject when the conversation continued.

City team

In terms of general attitudes and actions to 'deserving' and 'undeserving' poor, few comments or behaviours were observed in the City team. In terms of the social/psychological model the subjective norm of the City team towards judging who should and should not receive financial benefits on 'deserving'/'undeserving' grounds was very much against making such a distinction. However strong behavioural control in the workplace in terms of budgeting meant that choices had to be made about whom to give money to and without any other foundation for making such decisions moral choices were made and acted upon.

Silverton team

In the Silverton team, the women who worked as social workers, clerks and receptionists were mostly local, many of them from working class backgrounds, and most having to struggle themselves financially when their children were young. Subjective norms in the office included making jokey but judgmental comments about social service users in the area, most of whom they knew.

> Karen: They're wasters they are... they'd have to win the pools three times before they'd have any money left (deputy team leader, Silverton).

> Linda, a social work assistant felt that some people 'were just evil and used

other people', Tina, another social work assistant felt some users did 'con' social workers. Mary, the most qualified of the social workers in the team, talked about unemployed people as 'scroungers'. In the feedback team discussion at the end of the field work period, all agreed that poverty was 'awful' and that there should be no distinction between deserving and undeserving poor. However, individually in the same meeting, after the team leader had left, social workers told me 'horror' stories, almost competing as in the students' groups to tell the worst tale. Linda remembered the man who 'took from everyone and smirked', and Karen talked about a woman's house that was so filthy that she had to go first 'to show Carol (the new social worker) how not to stick to the carpet'. Unlike the student group, the tendency was to not pick the worst examples of poverty, but the worst examples of undeserving poor - people who were not grateful for what they were given, or who did not keep their house clean. However the comments were sometimes humorously made as if to avoid thinking about the reality of peoples' lives in these situations.

A social constructionist perspective might suggest these are stories told in the office to amuse but also to distance individuals from a job that was often harrowing and may have reminded the women of their own working class backgrounds. However the context also appeared to be judgmental and may have reinforced the team's social norms regarding people in the local community who could be labelled as 'undeserving'.

Mary - Silverton team

An in depth analysis of one of the female social workers in the Silverton team illustrates some of the dilemmas facing team members and how labelling some social service users and distancing oneself from such a group of people can be a means of avoiding emotional conflict. Mary was a part time social worker in the Silverton team. She was highly qualified for this post having a combined degree and CQSW. She had a generally negative attitude to people coming to social services with financial problems, assuming they were 'trying it on'.

However Mary had a caring attitude to her caseload clients and was not only aware of but prepared to help those with low income. Her personal situation was to some extent in conflict with her work responsibilities. She was married to a company director and her son was at a public school. Her husband had offered to give her the equivalent amount to three years in her part time job if she left, but she wished to maintain her work interests. In relation to the social/psychological model, her subjective norms at home with her family and neighbours were very different from those she encountered at work. The attitudes of her family and friends appeared to be that those who depended on the welfare state were undeserving whereas on a day to day basis she was coming into contact with people in poverty and work colleagues who had very different views. Although she appeared genuinely sympathetic to users on her caseload, in terms of subjective norms and perceived behavioural control from home, it was easier for her to disassociate herself from users with financial problems on the duty desk by labelling them as 'scroungers'.

Financial problems - deserving of social work time?

Many of the social workers in the two teams, saw work on the duty desk as less important, less 'deserving' of their time than statutory child care work and their caseloads. From a social service users' perspective telephoning social services or going to a social service waiting room and asking for help was very important. Hill et al (1984) note that the majority of social workers only became involved in financial problems because social service users brought the problems to them and not because social workers felt them to be an important part of their work. As Beresford and Croft (1993, p.50) note 'They (users) want services which respond to their needs, which consult with them, in which they have a say and sometimes which they run themselves.'

Social service users have a right to a minimum level of income and need policies, programmes and strategies to achieve that and social workers may be able to help in this process. From a social constructionist perspective social workers' accounts which define users as 'undeserving' may include all users who are not in a casework or care management relationship with a social worker, because this version of events has the purpose of constructing social work as social workers wish to perform it. Alternative accounts of social work constructed by users and carers, managers, the DSS, the government or social work academics might have a different purpose.

Research findings - welfare benefits

These fieldwork findings and others (Hill et al 1984, Wilson 1988, Becker 1997) show that there is a substantial gap between the theory regarding the need for practical help and welfare rights advice and advocacy and social workers' actual practice. Little benefits advice and hardly any benefits advocacy was observed during the thirteen months field observation with two social work teams.

The social psychological model

In terms of the theory of Planned Behaviour, it could be argued that social workers' attitude towards poverty was positive but that subjective norms of colleagues, team leaders and higher management tended to recognize for example, excellence in statutory child care work rather than the relief of poverty as an indication of a 'good' social worker. Perceived behavioural control in the teams was not only evidenced by opinions of management towards welfare rights but also by the pressure of high caseloads with little time and energy to perform all the statutory requirements required in each case. For example Silverton team had an on-going dispute with headquarters regarding the amount of casework they were expected to do especially with two members of the team off work with long term ill health and had resorted to 'stacking' cases (i.e. noting the cases allocated to them but only tackling those they had time for), and restricting by half the times when social service users could see social workers on the duty desk. As the referrals from the duty desk were more likely to be financial than referrals from other professionals, this also restricted the time they would be able to spend on welfare rights related issues.

Silverton team

The DSS policy of involving social workers in community care grants decisions had meant for the Silverton team a non cooperation policy in dealing with Social Fund issues and as a consequence some team members had little knowledge of this area. Although Vernon's comments in the fieldwork appeared to be directed towards social workers not being involved with income maintenance, he did not take part in a three day training course on welfare rights for team leaders. This disappointed the welfare rights officer Brian Lunt as he notes in a letter to the researcher,

> Welfare rights staff spent a great deal of time putting together a comprehensive training course for team leaders over a three day period. It was here that we found indifference and absence from some team leaders (Silverton). Other team leaders were enthusiastic and eager to gain information to pass on to colleagues at team level. I feel that team leaders' advice to social workers not to 'cooperate' with the DSS has been harmful to the so called 'generic' and 'holistic' approach to the point that now team members positively steer clear of benefits related issues and indeed are 'fearful' of becoming entangled in the system for fear of being exposed as de-skilled in this area. We have referrals for such routine matters as the completion of benefit claim forms. (Appendix 2).

The conflict between attitudes and actions in the Silverton team was concerned with having positive attitudes to poverty and negative attitudes in some cases to welfare rights and in other cases to income maintenance. Actions in relation to users were concerned with giving out money, clothes or food vouchers but not working with users to claim what they were entitled to. Many users with benefit problems were referred to the local welfare rights adviser, by the secretarial staff as well as the social workers. This created problems for Brian Lunt, because he was often busy with appeals cases and had only Malcolm, an unemployed volunteer who Brian had trained himself, to help him.

City team

Conflict in the City team was more likely to be concerned with positive attitudes towards welfare rights, but being able to do very little in practice. Perceived behavioural control from management which usually involved statutory cases was stronger than the pressure for help from users with financial problems. However social workers did have to respond to the pressure from 'below'. Some staff in City team tended to respond by being sarcastic. At a team meeting a woman was discussed who had made ten Social Fund applications.

> Theresa: I don't believe her any more ... She might not want money, she might want counselling. (Others in the team laugh) ... She's coming in, will say she's lost her money and threatens she wants her kids taken into care if she doesn't get help.

Theresa wanted to take the children into care but Bernard, the team leader said that, 'Those higher up might not appreciate it'. Theresa's humour seemed to be reserved for the office, for whenever I accompanied her on visits she dealt with welfare rights enquiries sympathetically and efficiently, including showing concern for the woman who had made so many Social Fund applications.

Stewart and Stewart's (1991) study of 1,200 clients referred by 226 social work teams in the 21 participating local authorities, reported negative attitudes to the Social Fund in particular as common among social work teams.

Benefits checks

I was expecting social workers to be conducting basic benefits checks when they saw social service users in the duty room and possibly on their first visit to a new client. I did not observe one benefits check in thirteen months. As Hill, Tolan, and Smith found in 1984, social workers rarely check users' entitlements to benefits. Leaper (1988, p.98) suggests referral forms might have helped social workers to check entitlement to benefit.

Of the 26 social services departments which responded with the forms used by social workers, only 8 per cent had any mention of the financial matters of the client. More authorities in fact recorded data on the religion or creed of client than on their financial situation.

Neither Silverton nor City referral forms included queries about users' financial status nor for example a box that could have been ticked to say that users' entitlement to benefits had been checked. During the period of the field observation, there was only one significant example of a benefits check that resulted in a successful back payment to a social service user. The welfare rights officer and social work assistant from Silverton challenged the DSS on their refusal to pay child benefit to Fiona, a woman with learning difficulties and her child. They won the case and Fiona received back payments of over £300 which she used to take herself, her son and her mother to Butlins for a week. This participant observation study found that welfare rights appeared to be an area of work that social workers generally did not do and did not want to do, whereas although they also may not want to be involved in income maintenance and/or debt counselling, they *were* of necessity on a daily basis.

Conclusions

In Figure 6.1 previous research has been characterised as being based around different epistemological concerns. Becker (1997), Parsloe and Stevenson (1978), Wilson (1988) and others have described social workers' attitudes to poverty and welfare rights as individual, preformed and relatively static. These researchers have used mainly quantitative methods or structured interviews to suggest how social workers respond to poverty issues. This type of approach is defined as 'snapshot' in that it fixes the data in terms of a particular time and place.

Other researchers who have not been solely concerned with understanding social work responses to poverty (Satyamurti 1981, Smith 1980, and Pithouse 1987), have developed a methodology and theoretical framework based on the idea that social workers' knowledge and ideologies cannot be measured in objective ways but are based on subjective interactions with others which vary from time to time and place to place.

By using methodologies that explore the more objective 'snapshot' approach (questionnaire, group discussion and interviews), and also the subjective interactive approach (thirteen months participant observation), this research has been able to demonstrate an understanding of the value and use of both epistemological frameworks. By applying theoretical constructs that understand attitudes and actions as being fixed concepts (the theory of planned behaviour) or that attitudes and actions are both behaviours and can be appreciated best from a more fluid interactive base (social constructionists theory), it is envisaged that this research has developed a knowledge and understanding of social workers' attitudes and actions in relation to poverty that integrates and develops previous findings on the relationship between poverty and social work.

Social constructionists theory and social psychological theories on the relationship between attitudes and actions are not complementary but rather in epistemological opposition to each other. However it is suggested that social constructionist theory and social psychological theory can develop our understanding of why social workers behave as they do in relation to poverty issues, and that the purpose of using two alternative theoretical frameworks concerning attitudes and actions is so that the reader can understand how each of the models 'fits' the fieldwork findings in different ways and in different places.

7 Social service users with financial difficulties - their responses

This chapter examines users' and carers' situations, their satisfactions and dissatisfactions and their suggestions for improvement of the service provided for them. Field observations are included but further independent evidence from users and carers is introduced through in depth interviews. Eighteen in depth interviews were conducted with twenty two social service users (see Appendix 3). Some were followed through from participant observations, others were chosen at random from the social services referral book where their reason for coming to social services was 'financial difficulties' and some were recommended for interviews by individual social workers. Where there was fieldwork data and observed contacts with the social worker, the social worker's attitudes and actions towards the user are compared with the user's perception of the social worker.

Power and authority

Although all interviewees were assured of confidentiality and anonymity, and despite the advantage of being interviewed in their own homes, social service users initially appeared inhibited. They were worried that the researcher was investigating on behalf of the Social services department (SSD) and/or the Department of Social Security (DSS). If the interviews had been with middle class people or those from an elite group in society, they would probably be less nervous *if* they agreed to be interviewed at all (see Chapter 3). However the fact that the interviews were about users' financial difficulties and asking for help would make most interviewees uncomfortable whatever their class and background.

The issue of the control that those in positions of authority exert over those they are providing a service for was evident in most of the interviews conducted. Whether those considered by users to be in positions of authority were social workers, DSS officials or even researchers and whether their 'control' was intended or unintended was not relevant. Social service users sometimes adopted a passive approach both in interviews (Wilson 1993, Dowling 1996) and in the observed interactions in the fieldwork. Other individuals used the interview to get further advice or to mediate between themselves and social services.

There was little interaction with groups of users in the two fieldwork areas studied although user groups are developing in many parts of the country (Peponis 1995). A development of this work would be to extend the ethnographic study of social work teams to social service users and carers. This could be achieved through working intensively with a group of social service users and carers over a similar length of time (13 months) to that spent working with social workers. Community care forums, user or carer groups, tenants group or community organisations would form a useful networking tool for this type of work and could be researched alongside users and carers. Ethnographic studies have been extremely effective in understanding: the views of young people on the streets (Parker 1974, France 1995), pupils in schools (Willis 1993) and mental hospital patients (Goffman 1990) to give but a few examples.

Characteristics of social service users interviewed

Users observed in the waiting room, on duty and out on visits with social workers ranged from a 16 year old black girl who had been ejected from the home of her adoptive parents, to an older woman alone in her flat who could not move from her bed. Young people and parents tended to discuss their money problems while older people did not. The interviewees contacted through the referral book tended to have occasional one-off contact with a social worker - when they were having financial difficulties. Eleven out of twenty two interviewees were women on their own with children dependent on income support. Six users tended to have long term contact with social workers. Of twenty two users interviewed, three were couples with children, one a couple with learning difficulties, twelve were women, mostly on their own with children, and two were male lone parents .Few older people were included in the referral statistics as having financial problems.

Low numbers of older people contacting social services regarding financial difficulties have also been found by other researchers in studying the effect of the Social Fund on social service users (Becker and Silburn 1991). Stewart and Stewart (1991, p.16) found in evaluating social workers' reports on 1,200 users using the Social Fund from 226 social work teams:

> the proportion of pensioners was surprisingly low, considering the prevalence of poverty in old age and particularly in view of SSD's responsibility for providing 'community care' services, which brings large numbers of people into contact with that agency.

However there were older people such as Mrs Merrivale observed in the fieldwork. They were not part of the referral statistics and while not asking for financial help were clearly having difficulties with their finances.

Mrs Merrivale

Mrs Merrivale lived on her own and had become anxious and confused about her money. All her bills, including her TV rental she paid months in advance. The manager of the TV rental shop had rung Tina, the social work assistant who looked after her, to say she was at that time twelve months in advance with her rental because she would forget she had paid and pay again. I observed two visits to Mrs Merrivale with Tina and was aware that here was a social service user who had fairly large amounts of money stashed around the house, which she had forgotten about. Tina and the home help had found some of the money (over £1000) while Mrs Merrivale was in hospital and put it in her Building Society account. On the second visit she gave Tina £5 to buy some fish and chips but became confused about the change. The aim of the social worker and the home help was to enable this lady to stay in the community where she wanted to be. However her dependency on them rather than an institution led to their controlling role in relation to her money and left Tina and the home help vulnerable in their positions as public employees to accusations of financial abuse (Bradley and Manthorpe 1997).

Satisfactions of social service users

Most users were satisfied when they asked for and received practical help or advice. With financial queries this could involve mediating with the gas and electricity boards, DSS, or other council departments such as housing or Council tax. The majority of social service users interviewed had short term financial crises with which they needed immediate help. They did not see themselves as dependent on social services, but were prepared to contact them in an emergency. In many authorities social workers are no longer involved in routine duty work such as this but for Silverton and City teams, it was a useful service particularly for parents who were having difficulties where children were at risk. The new Government initiatives for lone parents on employment and for families on preventing or coping with family breakdown (Sure Start) have highlighted the importance of addressing poverty. However at the present time the role of social work in these new initiatives is unclear.

Not surprisingly users were influenced by previous experience of social workers. If previous experiences of social workers had been positive, they expected and often achieved satisfactory help with a financial problem.

Mrs Crill

Mrs Crill was a lone parent looking after her two boys. Her two girls were living with their father. She found it extremely difficult to manage on income support and had contacted social services about her debts. She first came to social services about the possible sexual abuse of her boys by another boy.

> Mrs Crill: He (John, a social worker from the Silverton team) came up to see them. He were really good...
>
> Researcher: So really having done all that with social services to go about the gas bill wasn't really...I mean it's not the same.
>
> Mrs Crill: No but they are helpful social services, really helpful.
>
> Researcher: So you've not had any problems?
>
> Mrs Crill: No problems at all.

Mrs Crill had used social services to mediate for her on a number of occasions with the gas and electricity boards and DSS. However since her ex-husband had put her in touch with Brian the local welfare rights officer, she had decided to use him in future. She still was not sure what were appropriate concerns for social services and asked whether she should report her ex husband and his girlfriend because her girls and the girlfriend's older boys were sleeping in the same room.

Vera

Vera was a 16 year old ward of court, estranged from her mother and staying with her 19 year old friend Joan. Vera was not entitled to income support and had asked social services for financial help.

Because her mother regularly beat her up, and she was separated from her father, Vera had a social worker (Mrs Stevenson) for seven years before moving to the Silverton area to live with a friend Joan.

> Vera: She (social worker) were like an auntie to me. If I needed any money, any clothes, she'd get them for me. She'd talk to me. She'd sit there and listen to me while I were having problems. She were brilliant...she's not like a social worker, she's just like a friend.

This experience meant her expectations of a social worker from Silverton were high.

> Researcher: But what were you expecting when you moved here for the social workers to do?
>
> Vera: To be like Mrs Stephenson.

Joan, although only three years older than Vera, dominated the interview.

> Joan: I don't like any social workers. I'm not saying I don't like the people. I don't like the things what they do. I just think they're nosey. They interfere a lot.

Vera wanted a similar 'auntie' relationship to the one she had experienced before, but was constrained by living in the house of someone who had negative experiences of social workers.

> Vera: If I got to know a woman and got to trust her like I have Mrs Stephenson then I'd go down there and talk to her and see if she could help me like. But Joan - that's what Joan's here for. I talk to her. You're like a social worker to me! (We all laugh)...
>
> Researcher: If you had a problem would you go back to social services?
>
> Vera: Yeh, if it was one that Joan couldn't help me with. If it was a small problem then No I wouldn't - me and Joan would sort it out. But if it were a big one that Joan couldn't sort out then I would.
>
> Joan: Nowt I can't sort out! (Everyone laughs).

As the interview finished, Vera asked if they could send a female social worker out to see her. She had been to the town hall and seen the male social worker on duty but had not mentioned that she was hoping to see a female.

> Vera: ... I was trying to get to me mother to stop him (stepfather) from hitting her and she (the social worker) pushed me back and told me to leave him alone and I saw it all. (break in voice). And I've just been scared of men - won't talk to them, not unless I get to know them.

Joan then told Vera which female social worker at Silverton she should see - Beverley - because she was young and trendy and had helped her mother-in-law with a practical problem. The discussion over which social worker Vera should ask for was unusual. However middle class people are likely to have similar discussions about which dentist or doctor they should see. Why does it seem surprising that working class people want some choice over their social worker? I took the message back to the Silverton team (with Vera's consent), that Vera would like a female social worker and a particular one at that. However the team leader informed me that it was not their case and would stay with Mrs Stevenson's area. Mrs Stevenson was on long term sick leave. Vera did not appear to realise she was calling at the wrong social services offices. Although she was very satisfied with past social services help she had received, her current emotional and financial needs were more likely to be fulfilled by her friend Joan than Silverton social services.

Mrs Routledge

A minority of users - Mrs Routledge's situation is illustrative of a number of other individuals - had become social work 'cases' with financial difficulties as their main problem. They were often grateful for the help they had received over years. Mrs Routledge was on her own with four children. Her ex husband, a milkman, had stopped paying the bills and burnt the evidence. She was left owing £1003 to the gas board and £700 to the electricity board. She withdrew all her savings and insurance (£300) to pay off some of the debts. The gas was cut off and she had 'three bad winters with no heating at all.' Her husband had 'always been bad with money'. The worst period was when she injured her fingers and was off work as a cleaner for eighteen weeks. The social worker suggested she claimed sickness benefit from social security but she 'only got £4 then' because her ex husband was supposed to be paying her maintenance. He owes £700 but has 'got no money to pay it'. She has not been able to buy clothes, 'depends on what people give her'. Her oldest daughter had now got a mortgage 'one less for mum to worry about' is what she had said to her mother. The daughter had paid to have Mrs Routledge's hall and front room decorated, which were in stark contrast to the rest of the house. Mr Routledge had now moved out of their council house. When they separated he lived in an upstairs room while Mrs Routledge and the four children lived in the rest of the house. Her husband expected her to continue to clean, wash and wash up for him, as well as pay his debts. The housing department had told her to stop clearing up after her ex-husband and paying his debts. She kept paying the rent because she wanted to 'fight for my own house'. Eventually the family was evicted from their council house at 12 pm and Mrs Routledge without her husband retrieved the keys at 4.30 pm on the same day as the sole tenant. Brian, the welfare rights worker and John the social worker had been involved in helping her for three years. As Mrs Routledge explained, she was very grateful to her social worker, 'I don't know what I'd have done without John - much worse - be in the river by now.'

Mr and Mrs Partridge

Mr and Mrs Partridge, whose child had been in hospital, had mixed feelings about whether they were satisfied with their visit to social services. They had asked for financial help from social services because DSS had refused them help. They had been visiting their three year old daughter who was in a City hospital every day. It was costing them £5 a day in petrol and expenses from Silverton. As Mr Partridge was unemployed they had no money left to feed their other two children and themselves. Mr Partridge phoned social security and they said 'there was no way they could help with travelling expenses to hospital'.

> Mrs Partridge: He asked for like a loan. We needed help from somewhere so I said 'nip to social services to see what they can do for us'. They couldn't help us by giving us any money or anything but advised us that DSS can help.
>
> Interviewer: Were you satisfied with what happened when you went to social services?
>
> Mrs Partridge: Not for the first five or ten minutes when they kept saying that no-one could help me but after that everything seemed to be O.K. I think if we'd not asked it calmer a little bit, we could have come home without nothing. We'd have to go back Monday or Tuesday...but without losing his temper an all - he's not one for losing his temper all that much - but with sitting there and trying to explain to young lassie - she was helpful enough don't get me wrong - she was trying to be as helpful as what she can ...she didn't actually know 'owt

about this loan...and we slowed down and tried to explain more to her - she goes 'I'll see what they say but I can't promise you nothing' and then we waited and then everything was smashing.

Because the Silverton team had a policy of non co-operation with the Social Fund, Beverley the social worker concerned would have had to find out more about the loan system.

The majority of the social service users and carers observed and interviewed were satisfied with the advice, support and material help they received from social services. Only those with financial difficulties were included as part of this research study so their satisfactions cannot be compared with others who received a different sort of service. It may be easier for users to make a judgement about help with material needs where there is concrete evidence. However dealing with emotional *and* practical needs was an important part of the social work service offered in some of the situations cited from the fieldwork.

Dissatisfactions of social service users

If there was little or no previous experience of social workers or knowledge of what they do, apart from what neighbours or a friend have told them, users and carers have limited criteria by which to measure their satisfactions or dissatisfactions. Nor are there objective standards of good social work practice for users and carers to evaluate the service provided.

Mrs Frank

Mrs Frank had been to social services to see if she could get some financial help or advice while her husband was out of prison on home leave. She was on income support, had two children and no extra finances to support him at home.

> Researcher: Is that what you expected when you went down there?
>
> Mrs Frank: Well I didn't know really. I heard like he could claim something but I didn't know how true it was, and like his probation officer told me and like other people who have had the same experience as me and that saying it to me - so I thought I'd get in touch with a social worker and see if they could advise me.

Mrs Frank was told that social services could not help her. She did not pursue the matter as she had no evidence that financial help, preventive work or welfare rights advice were part of the social work task.

Mrs Routledge

Although finally satisfied with the help she received, Mrs Routledge had seen 'two or three social workers before' when she went to social services. They 'didn't do anything', had said 'come again if you want another talk', and 'we can't help you'. Her case notes confirmed that her two previous attempts to get help at the duty desk, had resulted in her being given advice and the file closed as NFA - 'no further action'. I asked Mrs Routledge why she had persevered, 'because of what other people said (her neighbours had suggested she should be able to get help from social services) and the arrears were more.'

Mr and Mrs Partridge

Initially Mr and Mrs Partridge were disappointed. They had expected direct financial help from social services rather than being passed back to social security who had already refused them a loan. However they persevered and were able to claim a Social Fund loan after their visit to social services. Not all individuals would have been as determined and patient as Mrs Routledge and Mr and Mrs Partridge in similar circumstances.

Other users with dissatisfactions felt that their money problems were not taken seriously and that they had to visit social services two or three times or become aggressive before getting help. Users who present themselves are often not taken as seriously as those referred by Doctors, Head Teachers, Health Visitors and the Courts (Davies 1985, p.19). With financial problems there is also the difficulty that these problems are not accepted as part of the social work task (Becker 1997).

Because financial deprivation is part of the environment in which social workers operate, can they become desensitized to individual users? Are social workers really aware of the financial and emotional pressure with which social service users are coping when they come to social services to ask for help? Financial problems are not necessarily seen as part of the social work task and they can appear time consuming and 'boring'. Users' poverty may be ignored or not taken as seriously as issues which are seen as more directly 'emotional'. For example a referral from a consultant surgeon discussed enthusiastically at a team meeting concerned a teenage boy who had been paralysed from the neck down after an accident while out playing. The surgeon thought that the family would need counselling concerning the boy's practical and emotional difficulties being back at home. The social work help he needed had statutory implications but so did Mrs Routledge's situation with four children and enormous debts. However it was only on her third self referral to social services that she got the help she needed. Being turned away when asking for help, waiting for long periods to be seen, not being given the relevant information and social workers asking too many questions were generally seen as criticisms of the system rather than the fault of individual social workers.

All of the social service users who had found out about Brian, the welfare rights worker at the Enterprise Centre since going to social services, said they would prefer to see him about financial problems. What users generally did *not* say directly was that going to social services, even if they were judged to be a 'deserving' poor person, felt stigmatising. As Davies (1985, p.18) notes, 'We know that virtually every visitor to a social service office feels some stigma in being there.' Perhaps they were not sure how social services could be less stigmatising, given its structure and roles.

On the other hand, welfare *rights* implies an exercising of power on the part of the user - getting their due - compared to seeing a social worker which implies that they have certain vulnerabilities

> Mrs Dale: A lot of people go to Enterprise now though, if they have trouble with the electric...You can say it to some of the social workers but I wouldn't to other people (that she had been to social services).
>
> Interviewer: You wouldn't mention it?
>
> Mrs Dale: I do now because people can be helpful can't they? But some people are looking down.

Mr and Mrs Baker

Mr and Mrs Baker were not satisfied with the service they received from social services because of the time it took the team to respond to their request and the lack of financial help offered to them. Their situation is explored in depth because it explores the clash in perspectives between the immediate needs of users and carers and the role of the social worker enmeshed in institutional and bureaucratic structures. It is also illustrative of other situations where communication between users, carers and the social services department broke down.

The Baker family already had four children when they agreed to take on at short notice Mr Baker's two nephews and niece. Mr Baker's sister and husband had split up and neither seemed to want to take responsibility for the children.

Mr Baker: She's (his sister) working in Safeways and only just manages to keep herself and pay the rent. Her husband's on social security and has disappeared.

Mr Baker took them on because, 'I don't want them to go into a home'. They had come to social services because they could not manage financially with an extra three children in the home. Mr Baker was working part time as a debt collector. They were claiming Family Credit but had found their financial support from this could not be altered for six months, despite their changes in circumstances. They had not yet received any child benefit for the three extra children and it was six weeks since they had come to stay. They had also been to Brian, the Welfare Rights Officer, who had told Mr Baker to give up his job and go on to social security as he could then claim allowances for the extra children. Mr Baker did not want to do this as he enjoyed his job and there was the prospect of promotion. The family appeared to have explored all the avenues by which they could get financial help to look after the children and had found none. Social services was their last resort.

By the time Karen - the social worker allocated to the case - visited them they already had considered in what ways they wanted help from social services. The nieces and nephew wanted to stay with their uncle. Compared to the cost and administrative time of the three children being taken into residential care, Mr Baker felt with his previous experience of foster homes as a child, that he was doing social services 'a favour' by preventing the children being received into care and therefore they should get some regular financial help from social services. Because of his childhood experiences he did *not* want his nephews and nieces to be placed in the same situation. Having waited two weeks to see a social worker it is understandable, in their stressed state, that the Bakers were disappointed by the arrival of a food voucher. In some social services departments including the City Team, the Bakers could have been paid to foster the children rather than them going into care, subject to social services requirements for fostering. Karen was very busy and had hoped 'she would not get this one'. The Bakers had telephoned social services three times after their initial visit and she had telephoned them once. I had interviewed them during the time they were waiting to see a social worker, not realising that their problem was still on-going. They seemed very anxious at having to wait as they had a number of unpaid bills because of the extra demands from the children. Karen's visit was not observed but I discussed the situation with her before and after the visit. Before the visit she commented,

Karen: Vernon (the teamleader) is not keen to give them more (than a £20 food voucher) as he feels the children should go back to their parents in Skegness. I feel he's being a bit hard.

When she came back she said:

> Karen: I took them round what I promised but they didn't like me asking lots of questions. I said I needed to account for the food voucher money. When they found that's all they were getting from social services, the wife blew up and told me to take the food voucher and clothes back. They didn't want charity etc. I managed to calm them down, turned my back on the husband and said to the wife, 'won't you please take this. £20 is not to be sneezed at'. She snatched the voucher back and started going through the clothes saying 'It's trousers I want' but then found the T shirts were good for her children. I said 'I don't mind what children have the clothes - give them away if you don't want them. I don't want to take them back to the car as I've got a bad back'... I've never had anyone throw a food voucher back in my face before!

Karen felt Mr and Mrs Baker were manipulative, 'not quite right, I don't trust them, something's going on there' and when she found the old records to show Mr Baker had been in care, this seemed to confirm her impression. The Bakers seemed more able and confident with authority than other social service users with financial problems that I had observed and interviewed. Vernon, the Silverton teamleader saw the Baker's problem from the perspective of a bureaucrat who has to limit scarce resources. He felt it was their choice to take on these extra children and that Mr Baker should have said no to looking after his sister's children if they could not afford to. They may have gone into residential care but it would have been in Skegness not in Silverton.

Being accepted as foster parents was not suggested to the family and very few families in Silverton were regularly supported by Section 17 payments or food vouchers. Unlike many people who came to social services with money problems, the Bakers did not adopt a passive role. They initially put their case in a direct, assertive way. As they waited for a response, received more information and finally were given a food voucher, their straight forward approach turned to anger and disappointment. As anger expressed in this way over a food voucher was not what Karen was expecting - people were usually grateful - she labelled them as deviant. Mr Baker's recognition that his sister was not able to look after the children was not recognized formally by social services and therefore the Baker's plan to prevent the children being taken into care was not taken seriously.

Summary

Experience of social services can give more insight into its working which in turn can give greater opportunity for user participation or assertiveness in the process. However the user's greater involvement in relation to social services can be viewed positively in terms of greater understanding, participation and assertiveness or negatively in terms of manipulation, aggressiveness and a lack of gratefulness. The Baker family, Karen the social worker and Vernon the Silverton Team leader had different social constructions of what the Baker's problem might be, and how it could be solved.

Participant observation in a social services waiting room

Another situation where users' construction of events was often different from social workers was in the social services waiting room. The conversation would usually start by somebody asking somebody else who they were 'seeing'- (which social worker). On a number of occasions I was asked who I was seeing and I would tell them the name of a social worker I knew. On this occasion, I initiated the discussion.

>Researcher: Who are you seeing?

>Michael: Ivan - met him nine years ago in hospital - the only thing he did then was to give me a lift home in his car - I don't suppose he's changed that much. I asked him about some money from the government 'cos I'm schizophrenic - he said 'I don't keep up with that sort of thing' and that's his job!

Michael had heard some information about community care grants, which his social worker in the City Team seems to have been unaware of - possibly because of the Team's policy of 'determined advocacy' in relation to the Social Fund.

All users whether interviewed or observed had no doubt that dealing with money problems was part of the social worker's job. Some users had been encouraged by neighbours, friends or probation officers to approach social services when they knew the person had financial difficulties. Probation officers have no resources similar to Section 17 monies to help families with financial difficulties. Social workers on the other hand, did not always see financial problems as an important part of their work. This is the misunderstanding between users and social workers which Mayer and Timms (1970) dub 'the clash in perspective' where social workers' training and subsequent attitude still emphasize caring and counselling for change, rather than the practical approach which users prefer.

Responding to financial deprivation and practical concerns could fit with the task centred or empowerment models of social work. It is what users and carers feel is an important part of the social work task.

How users would have liked social services to respond differently

In most interviews there was evidence that users were not sure what social workers actually do and therefore could not easily identify what they could do differently. Throughout one interview 'social services' and 'social security' were confused. Suggestions about what social workers could do differently emphasised practical caring help rather than 'control' which was seen as interference. As 19 year old Joan commented:

> Joan: They can do some good things. Like his mum's fetching up two twins and they're their daughter's twins and the social worker's been over to his mam. I agree on that, I don't agree on them coming out nosing...She was talking to his mum and she seems very nice and she got twin beds for them. His father's got thrombosis - has to have a car with tax, insurance - couldn't afford beds. She had no help whatsoever - so she went to social services and said she needed two beds and Beverley (social worker) got them.

Mrs Bagthorpe suggested social services should provide a list of privately rented accommodation so that women who had been battered and wanted to leave their husbands could go somewhere straight away rather than be taken to a women's' refuge. Previous to the problem with her mortgage (see chapter 2), she had tried to leave her husband and stayed a night in the women's' refuge where Linda the social work assistant had taken her.

> Mrs Bagthorpe: At least you could fetch a few belongings from your home - what you wanted without him arguing - get what bits you think you should have and removals and just go. You're more likely to stop if you've got things there.

Mrs Bagthorpe had said the Refuge was a cold and bare ex police station, that there was only one other woman there and that she had to baby-sit for four other children as well as her own three. She stayed one night and tried to claim income support the next day. She had her three children with her, it was pouring with rain and she had to get two buses to the DSS office. Eventually she gave up and went back to her own home and husband the same day.

From this research it seems that individual users are at an enormous disadvantage in choosing what they would like from services. If they are not aware of what organisations can or should do, it is extremely difficult for them to say how they would like social services to respond differently. The most common answer to the question of what would users like from social services was 'don't know'. User studies have pointed out that if a service exists *all* members of the public have an equal right to know about it (Davies 1994). General information on the structure and organisation of social services resourced by central government would mean that individuals had more knowledge of what social services can do for them before a crisis develops and social workers may receive less inappropriate referrals.

Social workers' attitudes and actions in comparison to users' views

Social workers tended to be more critical of users than users were of social workers. This may be due to 'letting off steam' which is part of any work situation. 'Service workers like teachers typically judge people they work with on the basis of how easy or difficult those people make it to get through a day's work' (Becker 1966, p.59).

Certain long term users with financial difficulties were seen as 'not likely to change' and in this sense were termed as 'undeserving' of social workers' time and energy (see chapter 6). For example Mary one of the qualified social workers at Silverton, was in the office at the time of Mrs Dixon's visit (see chapter 2). She pointed out how many social workers had tried to help Mrs Dixon and how hopeless her case was.

The social services' construction of the Partridge's problem was concerned with who was responsible for income maintenance in this situation. Vernon the teamleader advised Beverley the social worker on duty who was not sure what to do to send them back to the local DSS. She was reluctant because she said they had already been there and had got a pink form. The team leader said 'tell them to go back and tell them (DSS), they've got no money.' He had previously said that DSS enquiries are sent on to DSS and 'if they don't come back - presume it's O.K.' As a result of a team meeting discussing the research findings, what happens to these 'No Further Action' cases was debated. Although no new policies were put in place as a result of the discussion, social workers and administrative staff in the Silverton team became more aware of the issues that Fimister (1988, p.318) notes:

> There are also simple practicalities which, nevertheless, are of great importance to claimants as they seek a solution to their income

problems. Take as a notable example the question of referral procedures. In-service training (and information systems) should be sensitive both to agency policy as to when and in what circumstances it is appropriate to refer a case to another body; and to the location, procedures and opening hours of organisations to which claimants might be referred. This may seem obvious, but I receive with depressing regularity accounts of claimants who have been caused inconvenience, financial loss and general aggravation in being referred to the wrong building in the wrong part of town, or the right building when it is shut. 'Pot luck' referrals often originate, unhappily, from social services offices, confirming that training for good practice must sometimes concern itself with the most mundane of procedures, as well as with fine legal argument.

Life events

Stewart and Stewart (1991, p.28-29) suggest that 'life events' are the context for extreme financial problems.

> These events include: moving house, particularly without choice; changes in household structure such as birth or the death of a close relative, relationship breakdown, leaving the parental home; movement into or out of an institution; redundancy or unforeseen job loss; being the victim of a serious criminal offence or of a natural disaster such as fire or flood. Majorities of each survey population (in research on the Social Fund), were known to have recently experienced at least one such life event which had a bearing on their current financial situation.

For Richard and Jane a couple with learning disablities, there were at least five life events which had occurred within a comparatively short space of time - the breakdown of a previous relationship for Jane; movement out of prison for Richard and for both of them out of the hostel where they met; marriage; and two moves to their present address; and finally the birth of their baby.

Other users were also experiencing traumatic life events which affected their ability to cope financially - for many female users for example Mrs Crill, Mrs Routledge and Mrs Crale, this included the breakup of their marriage and caring for children on their own. Mrs Bagthorpe and Mr and Mrs Partridge had seriously ill children. Mrs Dixon suffered a bereavement and mental breakdown and had recently come out of an institution, and Mrs Frank's husband was coming out of prison and she was finding it hard to adjust to having him back.

Vera, at sixteen, had moved house and was estranged from her mother. As Stewart and Stewart (1991, p.29) note:

> There is a substantial body of existing research on life events, which has been conducted mainly from a psychological perspective and which largely ignores people's material circumstances and poverty issues (reviewed by Titterton 1986). Yet many of the events concerned can have the double effect of increasing the need for extra expenditure at the same time as reducing the person's income or command over other resources.

Key issues for social service users and carers

From the fieldwork and in depth interviews with social service users and carers, the following points need to be addressed in order to develop a more user friendly service and to establish the importance of practical and financial help for users and carers.

- Users' financial problems were often part of larger 'life events' that the individual is finding it difficult to cope with. These 'life events' were not usually understood as a potential underlying reason for the user's financial problems by the professionals involved.

- Dependence on social workers was preferable for women such as Mrs Routledge to dependence on an unreliable husband. For other women such as Mrs Bagthorpe, dependence on income support which she talked about wistfully, was preferable to staying with a violent husband which she did not talk about.

- Occasional social service users were often not clear how social services could have helped them in a different way. Social workers tended to regard these people as 'deserving poor' whereas people with financial problems over a longer period of time or who did not behave as expected tended to be seen as 'undeserving'. A problem solving 'creative' approach by users was not appreciated by professionals who did really not see themselves as in partnership with social service users. They appeared to expect users to be passive and require help.

- From a social psychological perspective (see Chapter 6) perceived behavioural control for social workers in dealing with the financial problems of users included: the priorities of higher management, budgetary limits and statutory work whereas perceived behavioural control for users included: having no food; fuel debts which could mean disconnection; and accommodation arrears that could jeopardize their home.

- Most users felt there was stigma attached to going to social services and stigma attached to having money problems. It was not clear whether users would have felt less stigmatised if they had been asking for social services help with problems that were not financial. Social workers sometimes appeared to take other problems more seriously than users' financial difficulties. There seemed little awareness from the social work teams of the prejudices which we all have towards 'deserving' and 'undeserving' poor.

- Most users and carers interviewed and observed thought that financial and practical help was one of the key tasks of social workers and they valued this sort of help enormously.

- Many users did not know or understand what services they were entitled to from social services. An initiative at government level is needed to inform individuals about the responsibilities of social services departments and their rights in relation to the services provided for them.

- Social workers were unaware of what had happened to social service users who had financial problems and were sent on to other agencies. Their referral forms were marked 'NFA' as if another agency was sorting out the problem when very little was known about what had happened in relation to the user's problem. There is a contrast between the power of the social worker to decide on 'NFA' without really knowing the outcome and the passivity and powerlessness of the user who has not been part of that decision. 'NFA' might solve the social worker's problem but does it solve the user's?

Conclusions

Of these issues, two need urgent attention. The lack of information and standards by which social service users can evaluate social work services is well documented in user and carer research (Dowling 1997, Wilson 1995). For all users in powerless positions, little will change unless a variety of communication and information systems are put in place to aid individuals to feel more in control of the services that are offered to them.

Secondly 'No Further Action' without effective evaluation of where individuals have been sent to and whether their concerns have been addressed is not an equitable way forward for social services departments. Integration of social services with other welfare agencies has been on a government and local authority 'wish list' for some time. Coordination, value for money and providing a seamless service for social service users is often discussed in relation to health, education, and juvenile justice. Social services departments also need to ensure they are working with social security departments to improve communication, minimise inconvenience and provide the best possible service for consumers.

8 Social work, poverty and social exclusion

In summing up the themes of this book and the findings from the field work, the issues that have arisen in the particular social work teams and local areas may not reflect reality in other parts of the country and other social work teams. Some social services departments have moved to a purchaser/provider spilt for all of their client groups while others have reorganised into specialist or community based teams. Many social services departments have administrative assistants screening self referred clients so that financial queries would be directed elsewhere without any contact with social workers or care managers. Nevertheless a participant observation study can show in an illustrative rather than representative fashion the range and depth of users' and carers' financial deprivation and the way these situations impinge on social work practice. This chapter suggests further social work education, practice, and research initiatives are needed to highlight and tackle discriminatory social work practices in relation to poor social service users.

Policies on poverty, social exclusion, community care and social services in the wider policy arena that are likely to have an effect on the future relationship between social work and poverty are examined and discussed. The restructuring of welfare continues but concepts of citizenship, social justice and the *equitable* balancing of private and public concerns will hopefully create a better future for social service users and carers.

Who are the users of social services who have financial difficulties and why are they poor?

This was the question posed in the introduction. From this study, female lone parents appear to be the most likely group to be *asking* for financial help from social services. Divorce or separation had significantly altered lone parents' financial status - the majority interviewed were living on income support and were prevented by their young children from earning, officially or unofficially. Where fathers were contributing maintenance, an equivalent amount was deducted from the mother's income support so they were no better off.

Lone parent families wanted independence through part time work plus help with child care, rather than through dependence on another male breadwinner (Bradshaw 1988). Such users did not see themselves as passively dependent on the welfare state. They had in reality active lives, where most were spending a large proportion of their time looking after children. They were unhappy at the level of benefit payments or the low wages they were surviving on, and that they had to ask for help from social services.

Other client groups in the fieldwork generally did not approach social services with financial need as their referring problem. However older people and people with disabilities would often approach their social worker for individual help with finances. Their financial difficulties were not ones that statute (Children Act 1989, Section 17) in England catered for. Scotland's legislation (Section 12) as far as financial need of social service users is concerned is more wide ranging (Davidson and Erskine 1992).

Generally users were poor because the level of benefit on which they were expected to live was inadequate for their needs and their need for housing could not be fulfilled by the private market. Social housing was extremely limited. Most social service users had exacerbated situations because of personal and family crises and were not aware of the restructuring of welfare that had limited their basic entitlement and their access to additional payments (see Chapters 2 and 7).

How do social work students and social workers negotiate with social service users and why are they dealt with in the ways described and analysed?

This second question from the introduction encompasses the purpose and aim in writing this book. From the 13 month participation observation period, interviews with service users with financial problems and the group discussions and survey findings with social work students, there were inconsistencies in both attitudes and actions towards social service users. Social workers' attitudes often did not correlate with their actions. Positive attitudes to aid those in poverty could be associated with negative actions - social workers became cynical and disillusioned by what they saw as obstacles from DSS and their own bureaucracy. Thus those with principled and positive attitudes to people in poverty could become resigned to doing nothing while those social workers who had in some cases quite hostile attitudes to users with financial problems, making pre-judgements about who was 'deserving' and 'undeserving' had a more pragmatic approach and could be more successful in their actions for users and carers. Social work students tended to have a principled and positive view of the relationship between poverty and social work which was consistent with their self reported actions in placement. However these attitudes and actions could change once they become established in work (see Chapters 4 and 5).

Chapter 1 suggests there is no one definition of social work or poverty. Hence the relationship between poverty and social work is ambiguous, and complicated. It is not surprising that attitudes of social work students and attitudes and actions of social workers were individual, confused and contradictory. A variety of actions were observed for dealing with a financial problem. They could include: counselling, giving or lending one's own money; organising Section 17 payments, handing out food or food vouchers; negotiating with DSS; giving welfare rights advice or referring the individual on to a welfare rights agency. Theoretical constructs for explaining individual inconsistencies include social psychological and social constructionist's views of behaviour. Individuals' attitudes and actions can also be situated within a wider institutional and policy context and these macro situations are discussed in Chapter 2. Social work education, government departments and social service departments give inconsistent and haphazard advice and instruction on dealing with the financial needs of social service users - none of which is coordinated on a national basis - later sections in this chapter deal with recommendations to change that situation.

Observing social workers over a long period of time, on a three or two day a week basis, has meant understanding something about them as individuals with strengths and weaknesses. Observations included informal situations, where social workers did not have to be on their best behaviour, or have the 'right' attitudes to poverty and social work. Most were unaware of the inconsistencies between their attitudes, beliefs and opinions and their actions in relation to poor users. However social workers see themselves as professionals, and their attitudes and actions in relation to the poor had a significant observed effect on users' lives. For this reason their power in relation to poverty issues has been highlighted and challenged.

Social workers and professionalism

Some commentators see the observed inconsistencies in social workers' attitudes, beliefs, values and actions in relation to poor users, as a product of professional discretion and autonomy, that social workers are well qualified 'experts' and like doctors and lawyers, they have earned the right to make decisions that are subjective, flexible and geared to the individual.

Four issues need to be addressed in countering this argument. Firstly, are social workers 'experts' on poverty related issues? The evidence in these chapters suggests they are not. Welfare rights, CAB and DSS offices are often overwhelmed by claimants' financial problems (Harrison 1983, Hill 1990, CAB 1998), and thus poor social service users cannot always be dealt with by organisations that are more expert. Social workers need to be aware of the impact poverty has on social service users' lives and to be alert to the opportunities for action that they have to support users in dealing with financial problems.

Secondly discretion is not the same as inconsistency. Professional discretion should be based on guide-lines so that individual users in similar circumstances receive similar treatment.

Thirdly as G.B.Shaw noted, 'professions are conspiracies against the laity'. Professional discretion can be a form of social control that prevents users from acting collectively and knowing what their rights are in relation to a social services departments.

Fourthly if social workers are to manage their resources and be responsible for what they spend (Griffiths 1988, NHS and Community Care Act 1990), a proper account of why, how much and to whom they : dispense Section 17 monies; support Social Fund applicants; purchase and provide community care monies and organise direct payments and grants from voluntary agencies is necessary.

A user's guide - information, guide-lines, accountability, access and participation

Social service users are not at present citizens with equal rights and power. They have very little information about what the service offers and are treated as clients who have decisions made for them by a social work service that feels it knows best and is doing the best for its users. If decisions are made on an arbitrary basis without rules, then social service users can only be passive. They have no rule book to refer to or right of appeal. They cannot be 'consumers' with a recognized complaints procedure. A clearly written, publicly available, policy for giving cash to social service users with guide-lines about how much can be given to each family, may in fact reduce the pressure on social workers for financial help.

A 'User's Guide' could include:

- regularly updated information on what kind of services are available, a definition of the criteria for being assessed as in high, medium or low need and a description of the process by which people can apply for services,
- clear and concise information on complaints procedures, Section 17 funds, the Social Fund, direct payments and charging policies;
- a section which advertises self help groups and independent and voluntary care organisations;
- accessible information on welfare benefits with telephone help lines provided for further information and support.

A guide such as this prepared on a national basis with local authorities providing their own local information would enable social service users and carers to uphold their rights as citizens rather than as passive recipients of services (Lister 1998).

The concept of a guide is not as far fetched as it may at first seem. A public management emphasis on users as consumers has encouraged the Employment Department for example, to change the term attached to those who are claiming unemployment benefit from claimants to 'clients' (UB40, 1990). The Department of Health sent a booklet through every household's door, (*The NHS Reforms and You*, July 1990), explaining the organisation of reformed health services and complaints procedures, so consumers are better informed in making choices about their health care. The Department of Education has encouraged parent participation in schools through the strengthening and codifying of the role of parent governors on governing bodies (Education (No. 2) Act 1986, Education Reform Act 1988).

Social services departments do not appear to have a similar nationally directed initiative to improve relationships with their user groups. Therefore although user and carer groups have developed, relationships with SSD's are still sometimes defensive rather than learning experiences for users, carers and professionals. Involving users and carers in planning and establishing a national user's guide to social services departments would be essential (Surrey User Network 1998). However guidelines to define social workers' role in relation to a whole range of issues could more easily involve users and carers when their association with social services is voluntary rather than compulsory (for example situations where there are problems concerned with child protection and acute mental health crisis).

Confidentiality

Linked to the issue of greater and more equal communication between social workers and users and less social control and stigmatising of poor users is the concern by social services departments about confidentiality. Although some social services departments now operate open access to files by users, such policies need to be expanded. Fieldwork files and referral forms in the research sometimes had comments that labelled users as 'deserving' or 'undeserving' poor. Confidentiality is a concern of the medical profession too, but it has not prevented greater access to information by users in health debates. With open access, social workers dealing with people who have financial problems would have to think more carefully about what is prejudicial or patronising in relation to poverty issues when writing up referral forms or reports. A textual analysis of reports and referrals on people who have come to social services with financial problems would make an interesting follow up study.

Cash and care

The idea of a poverty awareness programme depends on a philosophy that can integrate cash and care in considering social workers' responsibilities and duties. 'Cash' can be defined as all issues that relate to the material needs of users. This definition would include the controversy concerning whether social workers should be responsible for income maintenance, but would also include the debate about how social workers become involved in welfare rights issues and the practical provision of clothing and furniture. 'Care' can be defined as emotional support and counselling for social service users, but can also include statutory care which is necessary to protect children from abuse and community care so that users can live in their own homes in the community, rather than in institutional care.

Some social work academics would argue that it is not the concern of the social worker or the social work student to combat an unjust society and deal with the financial affairs of poor users. Poverty is hardly mentioned in statutory legislation which social workers must attend to. Pinker's perspective (Barclay Report 1982) suggests that social workers have neither the time nor resources to deal with anything other than the individuals they must deal with as part of their statutory obligations. This approach questions the assumption that because most social service users are poor (Becker, Macpherson 1988), social workers should be dealing with the problem. After all, DSS would not deal with a child abuse 'care' problem, however prevalent among DSS 'cash' claimants.

Arguing from a European perspective, Leaper's (1988, p.96) comparison of cash and care policies in Britain, Ireland, France and Belgium suggests that, on the contrary, social workers should be *more* involved with social security and income maintenance:

> What light do these references to other countries throw on the British cash and caring situation? First, it is clear that social work attitudes and practice can be integrated into the provisions of social assistance. In principle there is no real reason why DSS special case officers should not be trained and qualified social workers. Indeed if one were planning a really effective operation of a properly organised Social Fund for people with acute difficulties it would make good sense for Social Fund officers to have social worker training. Two essential provisos are: that decisions about entitlement are subject to review by some other body and that the basic income level for all in a clear and strictly enforced system makes discretionary grants (or loans) really exceptional. The British system of total nominal separation of cash and caring is an oddity, not a norm. We are the prisoners of our present system of administration which we disguise as a matter of principle.

There is a wide spectrum of ideas on how and to what extent social workers should be involved with users' poverty. The political left or right do not have a monopoly on either of these positions regarding more care and less cash or less cash and more care. Conservative government policy documents suggested that combining DSS and SSD functions would save not only the arbitrary division of cash and care in terms of responsibilities but also expense (Stewart and Stewart 1986, Alcock 1991b). Social work unions (UNISON and BASW) have been concerned that their members will be overloaded by short term income maintenance enquiries and have developed policies that in not cooperating with the Social Fund would appear to agree with Pinker's view that social workers should concentrate on casework.

Those who do not see dealing with poverty issues as part of the social worker's role would suggest other groups as being more effective in preventing or ameliorating poverty. Pressure groups such as CPAG, welfare rights officers, CAB workers and community workers are all involved in challenging DSS decisions and empowering poor people to fight their own battles. The Departments of Employment and Social Security, are of course the parts of the welfare state which were developed to ensure 'freedom from want' (Beveridge 1942).

Those who *do* see poverty issues as part of the social worker's role would argue that social workers are at the frontline of the misery, violence and abuse that poverty can create. They see the results of poverty and are one of the few professional groups concerned with deprivation still routinely visiting families and individuals now that DSS visiting officers have been virtually abolished. There may be nobody else that an individual with financial difficulties can go to, when for example sorting out the inefficiencies of the DSS. Voluntary agencies, CABs and welfare rights departments have been starved of resources, their funding is uncertain and they are inaccessible to the population in some parts of the country. Most importantly helping individuals with practical problems is what users want and appreciate (Mayer and Timms 1970, Sainsbury 1975, Davies 1985, Becker 1997) and what the general public considers an important part of the social work task (Weir 1981). It would be patronising to suggest that social service users could not benefit from the counselling that middle class people may receive (Laws 1991). However in terms of Maslow's hierarchy of needs, financial and practical help may be more immediately important than emotional support which may be given by family and friends and not needed from social workers. Nevertheless cash and care perspectives cannot really be placed in opposition to one another because as has been demonstrated in preceding chapters there are many complex and connecting links

If social services departments worked out clear policies on poverty issues that were accessible to users, money could empower users, rather than control their behaviour. A move in the direction of anti poverty policies would not only be preventative in terms of other social problems, but would give social workers a different, more positive relationship with users (Becker and Macpherson 1988). Social workers are defined by some users as being enforcement agents for laws which oppose them and involve taking their children into care or sectioning individuals who are mentally ill. In order for social workers to have a more equal relationship with users, where they are treated as citizens rather than 'clients', they need to feel supported in the area of their lives which are particularly important to them.

The theme of this book has been to suggest that the social worker's role does involve cash and care while recognising that the issues surrounding income maintenance are particularly hard to resolve for social services departments and individual social workers.

Social exclusion

Social exclusion is defined in this debate as being concerned with lack of income, resources and opportunities. Wealthy people may be excluded from the choices and opportunities that the majority enjoy because of age, disability, gender, sexual orientation, or race but poverty adds a crucial dimension to any form of social exclusion. Social service users and their carers are generally poor (Becker 1997). The wealthy generally pay for private care. Christopher Reeve or 'Superman' for example is severely disabled. Although he has highlighted the plight of disabled people in America in relation to the US welfare reforms, Christopher Reeve has choices and opportunities that many severely disabled people on a low income do not have. Most Labour Party policy documents and the Social Exclusion Unit itself tend not to define those in poverty as necessarily excluded. There are social exclusion initiatives for the homeless, school truancy and inner city areas. A wider brief constructing the country's poor as socially excluded would mean that social services and other public and voluntary agencies could develop a national policy for tackling deprivation. If the Social Exclusion Unit had been given their own resources instead of being dependent on the Treasury and other Government departments such a plan would be more likely to succeed. It is to be hoped that the Sure Start Unit which aims to work with parents and children to promote the physical, intellectual and social development of children from birth to four years old will use the £452 million given to them over three years to build lasting coalitions between health, social services, education and social security. However the positive benefits of *having* such Units that did not exist before 1997 cannot be underestimated. To achieve the best possible results they must not only speak up for the poor but *involve* them in decisions about combatting social exclusion, reviving poor neighbourhoods, and developing the potential of the nation's children (ATD Fourth World 1996).

Government policies on poverty, social exclusion and social services

A Labour Government was elected in May 1997 on a wave of popular support, similar to that for the post war government of 1945. If policy moves to ensure equality and opportunity are honoured, some of the poor may need social work less than they have done in the past.

In combination with the Social Exclusion and Sure Start Unit programmes, initiatives in health, education and social security are likely to have an input on social service users and carers. These include:

[Marks out of 10 in brackets are those given by Donald Hirsch, special advisor to the Rowntree Foundation on the effectiveness of these policies for the poor so far (Hirsch 1998)].
- the establishment of a minimum wage (8)
- the working families tax credit (8)
- working poor families £7-30 a week better off for those earning under £300 (8)

- small cut in national insurance contributions for the working poor (8)
- increased employment opportunities for lone parents, long term unemployed, young people and those with physical or mental disabilities (7)
- improved nursery provision for three year olds (5)
- investment in social housing, education, health, and employment action zones (5)
- investment in neighbourhood regeneration (5)
- non working families with young children receive £5 a week more (4)
- the reduction of VAT on fuel (4)
- £50 winter payments for poor pensioners (4)
- measures to improve pensioners take up of income support (4)
- increased child benefit
- a review of the workings of the Child Support Agency

Paid carers either working in social services, for voluntary or private companies or for individual social service users could also benefit from the establishment of a minimum wage. However there have been concerns about how the increased cost to the organisation will be passed on to users and carers. In the case of profit making concerns - for example the majority of private residential homes - they may have to go out of business, hike their charges to social services departments and private individuals and/or deny their workers other benefits such as paid holidays or pension schemes as a trade off for their higher take home pay. Individual service users on direct payments scheme will have to take responsibility for paying the minimum wage to their carers which may be at the expense of their own care unless this issue is taken into account by social services departments and the Government.

The Government say they must keep their election pledges on health, education, and employment and keep within the Tories spending plans for the next two years. They have pledged not to increase income tax which means as Hirsch notes (1998 p.20), '...higher earners have so far got off lightly. No increase in higher tax rates; no lifting of the cap on national insurance contributions, no restriction of tax relief on pension contributions, no further reduction in mortgage interest tax relief. The abolition of tax relief on private health insurance last year hardly made the pips squeak.'

It seems likely that social services and social security will be the 'poor relation' compared to other public welfare departments at least until May 1999. Labour Party manifestos prior to the General Election hardly mentioned social services and none of the five pledges were connected with social services. Policy documents on health and welfare make little specific mention of social services apart from the White Paper on social care whose publication date has been postponed. There are references to improved working between health and social services with pooled resources and budgets and an evaluation of the standards and quality of care provided (particularly for children and young people in residential care), but as yet no direction in terms of policy, commitment or resources (National Policy Forum 1998). Does the government believe that if they can reduce deprivation and social exclusion that there will be less need for social services and that SSD's responsibilities can be incorporated into education, health and social security?

Existing Legislation

The NHS and Community Care Act (1990) and the Direct Payments Act (1996) have laudable aims in giving individuals more choice over the sort of care they receive (although individuals with mental health problems or learning disabilities could not choose to stay in long stay residential homes). There appears to be an assumption that with greater choice, social service users can become more independent. The problem for social services staff, social service users and the public is that many users who are elderly, severely disabled or chronically mentally ill cannot transfer from being dependant to becoming independent of the services that enable them to carry on. Even users and carers who have less severe difficulties need help and support to prevent costly (for the user and carer and social services) crises developing. One also has to consider how choice can be an option for social service users involved in child protection proceedings and compulsory admission to mental hospital. It will be difficult for any political party to return to pre Social Fund days. The Labour Party may abolish Social Fund loans and restore the independent right of appeal in the Social Fund system, but are unlikely to re-introduce single payments. In this sense, the Social Security Act (1986) has changed the definition of need, it has restructured what was once claimed as of right and set a different agenda for considering social security in the future. It is no consolation for claimants that similar policies are being enacted in most capitalist countries and some that are socialist (Munday and Ely 1996).

Citizen's income

There are some indications that the Treasury is beginning to treat fiscal, occupational and welfare benefits as part of a whole package which individuals are entitled to throughout their life (McCormick and Oppenheim 1998, Mckay 1998). While the suggestion that any further rises in child benefit should be taxed is treating children as a taxable commodity, it represents a policy change from means testing benefits. Instead of social service users in difficult financial situations having to struggle with forms for means testing their benefits, those who are better off would be taxed on benefits which could include home care and respite care.

Giddens's (1998) thesis is that a 'third way' of governing that supports a social justice perspective while dealing with increasing globalization is needed It would not be part of the traditional left or right but would be suitable to centre left democratic parties (13 out of 15 ruling political parties in Europe). The idea of a citizen's income based on redistributive taxation - a full scale integration of the tax and benefit mechanisms - is suggested as an applied example of this philosophy. It has supporters on the left (Jordan 1987, Van Parijs 1992) and right (Parker and Sutherland 1994)of the political divide and would be an effective way of reducing poverty while avoiding the stigma of claiming benefits. The citizen's income would be paid to individuals not households, irrespective of any income from other sources and could be supplemented with paid employment - unlike the present welfare system participation in the labour market would always be positive - and individuals could cushion themselves against low paid, part time and intermittent employment. As Hirst (1998 p.81) notes,

> the prediction of the end of work may prove alarmist but in case it comes true it would be well to have experimented with guaranteed minimum income schemes so that their scales could be increased in the next two decades if necessary...a modest citizen's income scheme is affordable would have a marked effect on inequality and can be justified on grounds both of its administrative economy compared with targeted benefits and of social justice.

Summary

How will improvements in health, education and employment policies for social service users have a knock on effect in terms of poverty and inequality? Further research in relation to social service users and their carers would need to indicate to what extent they are benefiting from the new government policies and in what ways.

Not all 14 million people included in the government's definition of those in poverty (below half average income- 1993/4 figures) would choose to visit a social worker or would expect financial help as a result of being referred to social services. On the other hand those who are elderly and poor, mentally ill and poor, disabled and poor or who have young children and are poor have a double disadvantage and make up the great majority of those who ask for or who are referred for help from social services.

Community care - a redistribution of financial need?

Social services' role in community care and charging policies bring an unquantified number of wealthier users and carers into the cash and care debate (Bradley and Manthorpe 1997). Older people and their carers (whatever their income and social class) approach social services for an assessment regarding care in the community or residential care. If they have savings of less than sixteen thousand pounds and they are considered in high need, they will be entitled to help with the cost of residential care or care in the community. What is the impact of individuals from a variety of social classes approaching social services? For social services departments, it means an increasing number of referrals from highly vulnerable older people and their carers, not only for assessment of need but for advice and information on private residential homes and private home care agencies. With an aging population and increasing life expectation comes increasing frailty and increasing demand for health and social services care. Only 1 in 12 octogenarians are considered to be fully self sufficient. 'As medicine becomes better at rescuing imperilled lives and extending mortally threatened ones, the strain on resources will increase.' (Caplan 1998, p.21).

Charging for care

Can the Labour government tackle the controversial issue of charging users and carers for home care and respite care? It is justified by local authorities on the grounds that it has been necessary in order to accommodate the greater mix of community care users and carers and provides more overall care for the poorer members of the community. However is such a use of resources equitable in terms of financial and social need? Should individuals (more likely to be middle class) with savings who are charged for community care services pay towards those individuals without savings (more likely to be working class, women or from ethnic minorities)? LeGrand justifies his omission of personal social services from the 1982 analysis of who benefits from the welfare state on the grounds that there is no statistical evidence concerning social services distributional impact (1982, p.18) whereas Powell (1995, p 178) notes that there is evidence that personal social services are to some degree redistributive (Davies and Piachaud 1983). Charging policies could be identified as maintaining or extending the redistributive impact of public welfare policies in relation to community and respite care.

Charging for social is extremely controversial. One view is that people would rather pay through their taxes or national insurance contributions when they are working and well rather than when they are ill, older and not working. Other comments included, 'we don't charge for library books, why should we charge to have someone wipe our bottoms?.' and 'if the NHS can maintain a universal service - why can't social services?' Nevertheless social services departments in wealthy parts of the country but with poor resources for social services provision are able to increase their budgets considerably by charging for social care services, thus providing a greater level of service overall.

Who benefits from the welfare state?

Community care is an interesting example to consider in relation to who benefits from the welfare state because there is an interplay of fiscal and public welfare both in care in the community and long term residential care. Le Grand's (1997) article suggests that people who finance, operate and use the welfare state are no longer assumed to be 'knights'- public spirited altruists such as social workers or passive recipients of state largesse - 'pawns' such as social service users. All are considered to operate from a position of self interest -'knaves'. Charging for social care appears to encourage individuals who have saved all their lives to become 'knaves' rather than 'pawns' or 'knights'.

> ...it (means testing) encourages people to behave knavishly: to engage in means test avoidance, adjusting their means in such a way as to minimize the amount extracted by the state. What should be a noble act - the state helping those in need - becomes instead a sordid set of private activities of dubious morality and often even of doubtful legality (Le Grand 1997, p 165).

A small illustration of this private world of dubious morality was given to me by care managers in Surrey. They give examples of individuals who are admitted into private residential homes with savings of twenty thousand pounds. When four thousand of their savings have been spent, they apply for funding from social services, thereby being maintained in the private residential home of their choice without the need to be put on a waiting list (currently 10 months) for a place in a residential home. Those with less than sixteen thousand pounds in savings cannot 'queue jump'.

It has been assumed that social service users are less likely to benefit from tax cuts and tax reforms than the wealthier members of the population (Taylor Gooby and Papadakis 1985, Dowling 1993). However if wealthier individuals also become social service users, they are benefiting from the fiscal *and* public welfare systems. The question is whether social services aim to provide a service for the working class, the poor and those who are socially excluded or a universal service free at the point of access in the same way as the health service? Should social services care be for all members of the community or only for those without resources? These questions do not just apply to older people. Social Services Community care plans include services for people who are HIV positive, are refugees, have learning or physical disabilities or mental health difficulties and there are also community care services for children and families.

Universal versus selective services

With demand growing for social services resources - do we need to see individuals providing for their own social care needs where possible? If individuals were providing for their own needs where they could afford to, more resources could be available for preventive care which involved local neighbourhoods and self help groups. Better facilities could be provided for those with no resources of their own. This leads on to a series of other questions - if people with their own resources were providing for their own social care (as they now are for their children's higher education) - is it necessary for care managers and social workers to conduct assessments with them as the Community Care Act recommends? If social services 'screened out' all potential users who had for example savings in excess of sixteen thousand pounds, the resources saved could provide a better service for a smaller population. Community care services are currently allocated in terms of high medium or low need although some authorities are moving towards rationing services in terms of serious risk.

Ethical dilemmas

To assess for services only in terms of financial need could provoke serious ethical dilemmas for social workers and care managers. There would also be confusion in collaboration with the Health services presuming an open access policy for health needs continues. Community care principles mean that all individuals are assessed in terms of social need while health care assesses in terms of medical need. Financial need does not appear to enter the equation until after the assessment. This can lead to disappointment for users and carers if they are expecting a free social care service. Some individuals will choose not to pay and withdraw or minimize the service that is assessed as being needed. Carers who refuse a service on behalf of a user can be accused of putting the user at risk and users can be considered to be putting themselves at risk.

The arguments for social services provision to be universal and inclusive are strong - a non stigmatising service, in line with health service policies, a service that all members of the population can use, will feel proud of and be prepared to pay taxes to maintain. In order for such a service to exist, the government would need to provide the sort of resources that are currently being provided to the health service. Social services continues to draw the short straw in terms of being a service that everyone expects to fulfill their social care needs. Other government departments have either more resources to achieve similar aims (the health service) or have managed to divest their financial responsibilities for an area of need for older and disabled people which is growing in size (DSS). As Le Grand comments, 'The level of provision of community care is universally regarded as inadequate.'(1997, p.165)

The redistributive effect of community care is concerned with reclaiming monies for home care and residential care from wealthier users so that those without the same resources can benefit. The difficult questions in this debate are:

- whether in 'affluence testing' those who are eligible to apply for social services help, some wealthier individuals in high need would suffer. The sordid set of private activities that Le Grand fears are exacerbated with financial assessments at a time of crisis. Assessments could encourage neglect by relatives if they refuse to pay for the home care that the individual has been assessed by social services and the health services to need.
- whether the general public accepts a means tested community care service when the health service provides a service free at the point of delivery
- whether the loss of a universal care service would affect the status of the service and would further stigmatise individuals who did use the service
- whether social services can continue to provide with limited resources an adequate community care service for increasing social need and an ageing population.

Possible solutions - community care and financial need

The inequities of community care charging policies could best be ameliorated by ring fencing central government monies and redistributing them according to an equitable formula around the country. Redistributing tax and national insurance contributions to social services departments would contribute to a fairer society for social service users and their carers who are at present socially excluded. These suggestions are not concerned only with community care or social services but with equity, social justice and the philosophy of 'knights'

- reforms in capital taxes so that unearned income makes a bigger contribution to the system (Pile and O'Donnell 1997)
- reform of direct taxes so that they reflect ability to pay for example the

upper limit on national insurance contributions should be abolished
- reform of the social security system, including uprating benefits in line with earnings so that the incomes of the poor do not fall further behind the rest of society (Piachaud 1998)
- setting up a separate advice and inspection agency for older people which would investigate cases of financial abuse and monitor private home care agencies and residential homes
- The further development of government aided voluntary and private 'home from hospital' schemes to encourage individuals in their move either back to their own home or into residential care.
- Extended and realistic local authority and government funding for community care in both the health and social services sector so that preventative care can ameliorate some of the high risk situations that social service users and carers find themselves in.
- Funding of long term residential care to be 'affluence tested' but contributions to be matched pound for pound by the government. As Le Grand (1997) notes this would not constitute a redistributive policy on community care or long term care.
- Contributions for social service user's care from close relations as part of a legal welfare system - *obligation alimentaire* - as is the case in other European countries
- The development of a citizen's income so that the individual's fiscal and public benefits are combined

Social service users are generally defined as a socially excluded group in terms of lack of finances and opportunities for paying for private social care. However community care policies have also introduced wealthier social service users and carers into the debate. It is suggested that *if* these users and their carers are prepared to pay for their social care, social services can be seen to be operating as a redistributive service. Funding for increasing high social need can come through those who can afford to pay as well as through local and central government resources.

On the other hand if community care services are to be provided free at the point of access as health services are, then the government need to be convinced that they can raise taxes for this purpose and win a second general election. These issues need wider public debate and discussion.

Titmuss's (1968) illustration of the gift of (free) blood for the blood donor service as an analogy for how we can contribute to and get benefit from the welfare state without stigma is an example of everyone behaving as 'knights' in Le Grand's (1997) recent article. The depressing fact is that only 4 per cent of the population now regularly give blood to the blood donor service.

Although there are a number of reasons for the decline in donors, one wonders if Le Grand (1997) and Galbraith (1996) are right in suggesting a more selfish 'knave' population. If this is the case then providing adequate community care services will require affluence testing and charging policies.

However if Titmuss is right, that we are all concerned for social care services that we can contribute to and benefit from ('knights'), then the Government need to aim by the end of their first five year term to have increased the public's enthusiasm for funding universal services. If they are successful, then they can develop a strategy for how to utilise increased resources for the empowerment of social service users and carers within a social care framework.

Poverty awareness

Poverty awareness suggests that the position of the poor cannot be considered without considering the attitudes and actions of those in positions of power and wealth and how occupational and fiscal welfare increase financial security for only some sections of the population (Cook 1989). The ideas connected with poverty awareness are relevant for the majority of the population who do not see themselves as part of the problem. As Titmuss noted in 1968 (p.163) 'we have sought too diligently to find the causes of poverty among the poor and not in ourselves.' The issue here is that the poor as a discriminated group, whatever their age, disability, sex or race, need to be recognized and that training, policies, practices and laws can begin the process of creating a citizenship that does not exist for them at the present time (Lister 1998).

Social workers appear aware of poverty in theory and acknowledge it is an indisputable part of social service users' lives. In practice the fieldwork has suggested, they appear to find it difficult to translate attitudes into actions. Psychological models have suggested that subjective norms of others and perceived behavioural control in the workplace and in the wider environment will affect social workers' ability to turn attitudes into actions. The poverty awareness programme would ask students and in-service social workers to examine their own attitudes and actions and to understand how 'micropolitical' change may be possible in the workplace when macro-change is out of the question. 'Micropolitics' involves making small practical changes in methods of day-to-day working that may have significant consequences both for relationships with clients and for developing more effective modes of participative practice (Statham 1978).

By examining their own social construction of the relationship between poverty and social work, poverty awareness training could allow individuals to change their attitudes and behaviour so that they have a subject to subject relationship with poor users rather than a subject to object relationship which tends to increase users' feelings of social exclusion, marginalisation and worthlessness. There is no consensus either within or outside social work on the relationship between poverty and social work, and therefore the task of developing and implementing poverty awareness training becomes more difficult.

> What role should social workers have in relation to ever-worsening poverty? How much discretion should they be allowed in dealing with clients? How many of their clients assumed client status only because of chronic destitution? Were there ways of working with people in extreme poverty that enhanced their independence rather than reinforced their dependency? The wider role of social workers in enforcing social security regulations has only intensified the dilemmas that were originally encountered in the field of welfare rights. (Langan and Lee 1989, p.15)

Fimister (1988) and Alcock (1991b) suggest that income maintenance, welfare rights and debt counselling are all practice issues that social workers and welfare rights officers need to be prepared to deal with. Poverty awareness may be one contribution to preparing individual social workers and teams for social work practice in the next century.

Poverty is one area of social work that cannot be privatised, treated pluralistically or packaged. Treating poverty seriously may counteract feelings among social workers that they are coping with a rising tide of desperate people, that the rest of society does not even know about, let alone care about. By social workers becoming more aware of poverty, and being able to do something about it in the context of their work, there may be the opportunity for them to feel more positive about their work, and to combat the depressing feeling that social work is not valued because the people it is concerned with are not valued. This is an optimistic way to tackle the observed demoralisation in the social work teams. Some social workers did not see poverty as their problem and would not agree that dealing with it would help their sense of being undervalued. They believe themselves to be under resourced, overworked and overwhelmed by new policies and legislation. Preventative work on ameliorating poverty among social service users would not be their first priority.

What is suggested is that many social workers entered the profession out of a desire for justice as well as a desire to help. This is certainly evident from the social work students interviewed and surveyed. To emerge from the plethora of legislation, internal markets and demands of managers, to fight for the rights of users would remind social workers of their original aims in joining such a profession. A poverty awareness programme asks social workers to re-evaluate their own attitudes and actions to poverty, and would use participants' suggestions to find more positive ways of helping poor users.

With commitments from the programme, social workers could develop the 'quasi-customer' role of social service users in current legislation into a genuinely 'user friendly' service. As Langan (1993, p.158) comments:

> All the legislation highlights attempts to redress, at least rhetorically, the balance of power (and its implicit relationship of dependence) between the 'client' and the social worker. The main axes of this are the market/customer model in community care and the legal systems of scrutiny, appeal and complaint in child protection and mental health. In this respect, the changes have recognized some of the challenges from the margins to social work, although not necessarily in the forms that the challengers would have wished (Langan 1993, p.158).

Policy and research recommendations

Ideas and suggestions regarding the future of social work and its relationship to poverty and social exclusion are distributed throughout the book. These recommendations are important but not final and should be considered in relation to recommendations in other chapters.

- Poverty awareness programmes would need to be researched and evaluated if implemented as part of DipSW and other in-service training courses. These course development ideas have so far only been tested on groups of social work students as part of the research and as workshops and lectures to postgraduate students at the University of Sheffield and Royal Holloway, University of London.
- Social workers' relationship with DSS and welfare rights organisations needs to be defined and understood by all concerned. Small scale practical ways of dealing with income maintenance and welfare rights issues in collaboration with DSS, CAB, welfare rights agencies and social services departments would be a positive way forward. For example one of the Social Exclusion Initiative prizes was won by a CAB office in Sheffield involved in organising a mobile bus to deliver welfare rights advice and support to mental health service users on a particular estate. There is no reason why social services could not collaborate on these type of projects. Social workers need to develop ways in which access to social services and participation of users is encouraged.

- Textual analysis of social services referrals would highlight in more detail the way that poor social service users are discriminated against. Policy recommendations regarding the writing of case notes and referrals would need to take into account the open access to social service files practised by more and more social work teams. Referral forms that included details of social service users' financial status and/or work situation could be stigmatising for social service users however useful for research purposes. However if such forms also included a basic benefits check, it may be that this advantage to users would outweigh the disadvantage of disclosing personal information.
- Community social workers (of which I was one) were thought to have had their day in social services. However with the regeneration of deprived areas, it will be very important that social workers are working in and with neighbourhoods - that social services acts as a facilitator to put people in touch with self help groups and user and carer groups. As Drakeford (1998 p. 228) comments 'Care of the economically fragile which is rooted in a real rather than imaginary notion of 'community' would begin with the experience of those who know how their communities work, and how they could be helped to work better. There is a real role for professional workers in linking their service users to these networks and helping to ensure that they obtain access to the direct benefits for their financial circumstances which would follow.'

Concluding note

Not all that has been examined and debated can be summarised in this last chapter. If anything the final chapter has been a springboard for new ideas concerning inequalities in current social services' systems. If social services like the government is to find 'a third way' there must be closer working with:
- government departments such as DSS Health and Housing;
- private and voluntary organisations;
- social service users and carer organisations in local neighbourhoods.

There are a variety of ways in which social workers are still advocates for the poor and this role needs to be recognised in social work education, social work practice, the institutional culture of social services departments and government departments.

Appendix 1

The professionals in the study

Social workers and other social services staff observed, or discussed, during the fieldwork.

Silverton Team - Carshire Local Authority

Assistant Director	-	Geoff Harding
Divisional Officer	-	Barry Tomms
Teamleader	-	Vernon Rudd
Social workers	-	Karen (acting deputy teamleader)
(These social workers were present for some or all of the 9 month fieldwork observations)	-	Mary, Beverley, John, Tony, Carol Linda and Tina (social work assistants)
Shirley	-	newly appointed social worker who was present for some of the field observation period
Stephanie	-	off sick for most of observation period
Sarah	-	Deputy team leader off sick during observation period
Mrs Stephenson	-	social worker from another social work team discussed by Joan and Vera, social service users
Lorna	-	Home Help organizer
Edward Dent	-	Principal Welfare Rights Officer - Carshire Social Services Department
Brian Lunt	-	Local Welfare Rights Officer - Social Services Department
Malcolm	-	Volunteer assistant to Brian Lunt

City Team

Research Officer	-	Roger Plant
Teamleader	-	Bernard Sellars
Social Workers	-	Theresa, Dianne, Simon, Keith, Sheila Jane, Tim
(These social workers were present for some or all of the 4 month fieldwork	-	Tanya (Social Work Assistant) Maria (Administrative Officer)

period)
Centre '90 - Hostel for sex offenders
Ivan - Social worker from another social work team discussed by social service user in the waiting room.
Pete - Social worker from another social work team discussed by Jane and Richard, a couple with learning difficulties.

Appendix 2

An index of social service users referred to in the text

Silverton Team

Mrs Bagthorpe:	Married with a working husband and four children. Building Society had threatened to evict the family for mortgage arrears.
Marilyn Bagthorpe:	Mrs Bagthorpe's daughter with severe disabilities
Mrs Bailey:	Refused interview as her husband did not want to discuss their financial problems.
Mr & Mrs Baker:	Had four children of their own - one who was hyperactive. They had taken on Mr Baker's sister's three children, but needed financial help. Mr Baker had been in a children's home as a child and did not want this to happen to his sister's children. Mr Baker worked part-time and the family were claiming Family Credit.
Mr Butley:	Married with one son. Requiring help with rates bill.
Mrs Crale:	Lone parent on income support, with two children. A working husband in Saudi Arabia - however, she had recently separated from him. She had multiple debts caused by a sudden drop in income.
Mrs Crawley:	Married with two children, husband unemployed. She was enquiring about welfare benefits.
Mrs Crill:	Lone parent on income support with two boys - multiple debts. Her two girls lived with her ex-husband
Mrs Dale:	Young lone parent with one child. She had difficulty paying electricity bill.
Mrs Dixon:	Lone parent on income support with two children still living at home. She had a mental breakdown due to a sudden bereavement and her gas being cut off for a bill of £0.72.
Mr Farmer:	Lone parent on income support, with five children. Oldest stepson continually running away. Mr Farmer wanted to move, but owed rent on his council house.
Fiona:	Lone parent on income support with learning difficulties. She has a three year old child and lives with her brother and physically frail mother.

Mrs Frank:	Lone parent with two children on income support, whose husband was in prison.
Mr & Mrs Hallam:	An ex miner and his wife with six children. He had dropped the keys to their mortgaged property through the doors of the Building Society as they could not afford the repayments during the miners' strike. They left to live in a two bed-roomed Housing Association house.
Joan and Vera:	Two young women, one with three children. Vera had been to social services for financial help as she was under eighteen and separated from her mother (no income support).
Mrs Merrivale:	Older woman on her own - confused about her money - drawing a state pension.
Mr & Mrs Partridge:	On unemployment benefit and enquiring about financial help for visiting their sick child in the Children's Hospital 25 miles away.
Mrs Routledge:	Lone parent with two children, still living at home. Her ex-husband, a milkman, had built up enormous debts that she was unaware of. She had to pay the debts back out of her low wages as a cleaner.
Mrs Weller:	Lone parent on income support with two children, multiple debts.

City Team

Beatrice:	45 year old woman with learning difficulties living in a hostel - in multiple debt until social work assistant became involved and helped her to sort out her finances.
Mrs Crawford:	Lone parent on income support with four children under five - had been staying in a bed and breakfast for two weeks while awaiting a council flat in a high rise block. She had moved from a women's' refuge.
Mrs Grant:	Wanted help with bus fares taking her two grand-children to school, while her daughter was in prison. She had at that time no financial support from DSS or child benefit for them.
Mrs Holden:	Telephone request for a qualified social worker.
Mrs Howarth:	Telephone enquiry - wanted a social worker to remove a slug from her bathroom.

Joyce:	Married woman whose two children were thought not to be adequately clothed for nursery.
Jan and Richard:	Couple with learning difficulties who had problems managing their finances. Jan had had three children all of whom had been taken into care. They were called Rebecca (the oldest), Jonathan and Samantha.
June:	A woman with learning difficulties who had moved out of Rampton Hospital. She had been told by loan sharks she could buy her council flat with a £25 deposit.
Kate:	Lone parent with four children under five, had had twelve crisis loans from DSS.
Miss Lerner:	Could not manage on income support - had a two year old child.
Michael:	Had mental health problems, was waiting to see his social worker in the social services waiting room. He expected financial advice regarding DSS payments - but had not received any so far.
Mrs Quell:	Telephone enquiry about money for her child's coat (on income support).

Appendix 3

Feedback papers

Silverton Team
Meeting with Silverton Social Services Team - Participant Observation Study on Poverty and Social Work

Aims of the study:

1. To observe social workers' attitudes and actions in relation to poverty. Other research that has dealt with these issues has not documented social workers' actions. The methodology will highlight the relationship between attitudes and actions, thus being an original contribution to literature on poverty and social work.
2. There are few participant observation studies of social workers (three to my knowledge). This study could develop the use of participant observation as a method for a qualitative understanding of professionals' work within a team and within a larger organisation.

Work completed so far
Apart from just 'being around' for team members to get to know me and talk to me, I have carried out the following activities:

A. Identified from the Team's Referral book, referrals that are financial or non-financial and allocated or non-allocated. I have also attended team meetings where these referrals have been discussed.
B. Accompanied social workers on visits of all sorts, not necessarily related to poverty. I have changed offices so that I have been able to get to know all the social workers in the team. I have completed the following visits: Karen (5 visits); Tony (4 visits); Tina (4 visits); Linda (4 visits); John (2 visits). I have also been an observer when Mary, Tony, Karen (twice) and Carol (twice) have been on duty. I hope to have the opportunity to go out on visits with Mary, Beverley and Vernon.
C. I have conducted informal interviews with John, Tony, Karen, Linda and Beverley on what they feel is important about social work and poverty and still have to interview Vernon, Mary and Tina.

D. I have taken notes of team meetings (some written up for the team), attended meetings with outside agencies such as welfare rights and DSS (3 times) and have visited Carshire advice shop.
E. I have had three interviews with the divisional field officer and have been present when the assistant director has been talking to the team leader and another member of the team.
F. I have interviewed at their homes two women who John thought had particular problems with poverty and who were on his caseload and one on Linda's caseload.
G. I have followed up referrals on poverty which have been designated NFA (no further action).

Preliminary findings

These findings are more in the form of questions rather answers which I hope will stimulate an interesting discussion at the meeting. The hypotheses I had when I started this research were that social workers' attitudes to poverty would vary, depending on their background, education, political views, social mobility and their personal and financial situation. I suspected that these attitudes would influence their practice. Social workers' attitudes and actions have proved more complex in practice. Here are some anonymised examples:

Social worker A spent a number of hours on the telephone sorting out how a striking miner's family could receive benefits that had been refused by the local DSS. However she admitted that if she had had a full caseload she would probably have just told them to 're-present their bodies to DSS'. Even if this social worker's attitude to people with money problems is positive, how far will her actions be tempered by the amount of work she has?

Social worker B thinks some of the people who come to Social Services are 'scroungers'. She has difficulty dealing with benefit details although at home she does all her husband's book-keeping. I was aware when visiting a family with her how embarrassing dealing with money matters can be. Although the social worker's actions were positive in that she was enquiring whether the mother wished to claim benefits, the mother herself was uncomfortable and said her boyfriend didn't agree with it. If money like sex is a forbidden topic, is it possible for social workers to discuss it without compromising their relationship with the person? Is it something that has to be established in the relationship right from the start? Is discussing money seen by some people as socially controlling and an invasion of privacy?

Social worker C was dealing with an unemployed man in the duty room who she felt was manipulative and would be back again. She did not show this in her attitude to him, although there was a pregnant pause when he said he could not afford to take a job he had been offered because the pay was too low. It was only later when discussing the case with an unemployed friend that I worked out the financial details and realised he would be considerably worse off. How much does how rich or poor we are personally, affect our attitudes and actions?

Social worker D sees some individuals as 'undeserving' but in her practice seems particularly concerned to deal with money issues, including setting up welfare rights sessions at a local clinic. Are there individuals or groups who are 'undeserving'? Why? What do we mean when we define someone as poor?

Social worker E had given her own money to a mother who was in debt. The woman had got into debt for a number of reasons, but these included an oversight by the social worker and the welfare rights officer on an aspect of her benefits and an administrative mix up at the DSS. Do social workers feel they want to give money to people in individual cases? How do attitudes and actions link here?

Social Worker F took me on a visit where he saw the main problem as a teenager who continually ran away from home. He apologised because he did not know if I would be interested in a case that was not directly connected with poverty. In fact it was one of the visits I have found most shocking in terms of the poverty of the area and the family, in which the father had four other children to bring up on his own. His questions to the social worker were about money or feelings about his stepson. It must seem exciting to a teenager to get away from all this, especially to richer areas, homes and cars. The social worker and I agreed that there were financial implications for social services in bringing him back from where he had run to and that was a reason for social services returning the responsibility to his father. A runaway could come from a wealthy background too. What are our conceptions of poverty? How much of a social worker's caseload is to do with poverty and in what ways?

Social worker G has a sympathetic attitude to people with money problems but seems to feel they are problems for DSS to sort out. In a duty case an unemployed family had no money left to live on because they had spent it on fares to the hospital twice a day to see their youngest child. He suggested they re-present themselves to DSS who had given them a pink form that morning. How much of a social worker's role is and should be connected with poverty?

What is the relationship between social services and social security? How does the structure of social services fit in helping people who are poor?

The final question here must be how do we as social workers think our attitudes to poverty are connected to our actions?

Provisional conclusions

Social workers' attitudes to poverty appear somewhat disconnected from their actions. There have been several studies of social workers' attitudes to poverty but none to my knowledge of their actions in relation to poverty. If attitudes and actions are different, then researchers cannot automatically rely on surveys and interviews when making policy recommendations.

Being a participant observer has not always been easy. I am aware that no members of the team can act as if I am not there and I have appreciated their willingness to discuss what they are doing and why. This method of research will involve a discussion of how I have made decisions about being a passive observer or an active participant. The times when I have been more active in my approach may have affected the team members in their awareness of the relationship between poverty and social work (for example what effect will reading this paper have?).

Policy recommendations at this stage are tentative. Here are some ideas to which I would *welcome* feedback.

- As approximately 25 per cent of referrals are financial and designated NFA a duty officer who had extra training in welfare rights and whose sole responsibility was duty may help people who come in with straightforward enquiries. A limited caseload of people who had problems which included long term financial difficulties could make this work more interesting.

- Most social work cases that were observed involved poverty. A training day once a month where poverty related issues were discussed perhaps with members of the welfare rights team could prove useful for everyone. This would not necessarily be a welfare rights information giving session but a workshop/surgery where social workers could present cases connected with poverty that are proving problematic and hear advice or information from whoever was there. It could also provide a useful forum for discussing more general issues like the Social Fund or imminent changes in social security benefits.

City Team
Meeting with City Social Services Team - Participant Observation Study on Poverty and Social Work

Questions for discussion

1. All team members seem to work extremely hard and show care and concern for the people they are working with. It is difficult to quantify the number of cases each social worker deals with per day or per week as some cases come through the formal referral system, others through contacts such as G.P's and health visitors and others through the informal network on the patch. However the atmosphere in the team office is one of constant telephone calls and social workers rushing in and out from visits. How many cases would team members say they deal with per day or per week on average? What percentage come from the sources I have mentioned ? Are there any other sources?

2. Team members tend to respond quickly to calls for help. The administrative staff see this as sometimes causing referral problems. What exactly is the problem and can it be solved?

3. Most cases I observed had some connection with poverty. Social workers used Section 17 monies up to the £30 limit where they could. Any money spent or applications for example for a telephone have to be accounted for in increasingly bureaucratic ways due to overspending on the social services budget. I sensed some uneasiness about dealing with money issues. Were there criteria for deciding who to give Section 17 monies to and who should not have financial help? Giving out food vouchers or taking food round to some families rather than giving money seemed part of the system rather than what individuals in the team wanted to do. Is this a fair reflection of procedures and attitudes in the team?

4. I did not observe very much welfare rights work with clients. Is this because people use the welfare rights or advice centres for money problems? Social workers did however cooperate with DSS to obtain large community care grants for some people who were setting

themselves up in the community. Fostering allowances organised quickly for relatives of children that would otherwise be taken into care, seemed a useful procedure which I had not observed in other social services departments. How does this work in practice? Does it happen very often?

5. Clothes and toys presumably brought in to relieve hardship among clients, seemed instead to be creating extra confusion as files and papers (and the desk I was using!) got hidden underneath them. Social workers appeared too busy to distribute what had been donated. Are the toys/clothes distributed by anyone else? Have they been kept anywhere else?

6. Most of the team members have known each other and the area for a number of years. They seem relaxed and supportive to each other. There is no formal hierarchy within the team, and the teamleader is happy about team members taking responsibility for their actions, coming to him when they need advice. How does this set up work for new members of the team, students and researchers? How often are staff meetings normally?

7. It seemed difficult to communicate with the whole team and be sure they had got a message for example when I was ill. Is this the case for communications that have to be conveyed to everyone, for example policy decisions? Linked to this is the system for messages and referrals. Are there day books for both tables or are there differences in the system for the two groups of social workers?

Summary

Social workers in the team acted professionally although there was some evidence that social workers' attitudes are different from their actions in relation to poverty.

Why a team under siege? Apart from the constant pressure of the work, there is the feeling that higher management does not support this team's way of working. They did not succeed in getting an office that is based in the patch they are working and the new policy developments which are based on specialisms do not support a patch team in this area.

The structure of the social services department rather than the attitudes of individual team members seem to have the greatest effect on how social services do /do not alleviate poverty. What do team members think?

Team policy ideas for consideration

- A minuted team discussion on policy developments and where the City team should fit in could be arranged and the results sent to management.
- All toys/clothes could be stored in the waiting room and a sign put up suggesting people waiting help themselves.
- A once a month team meeting to tackle poverty issues with/without welfare rights workers could be arranged and individual cases could be presented, thus sharing advice and support in a more formal way. Newcomers and students could learn more about the contacts and networks that existed and the information exchanged could increase everyone's knowledge of the patch, its clients and its resources.

Appendix 4

Comments on the research by Brian Lunt, Welfare Rights Officer, Silverton

Extracts from a letter to the researcher are included here.

One social worker (Shirley) arrived as a new member of the team at Silverton. She was a working class woman who had experienced poverty first hand and had come into higher education and social work in her forties. She immediately made contact and joined CPAG and even participated in a residential course on Benefits. Within months the contact had reduced to purely 'crisis' cases and I discovered a change in her attitude. I realised that the influence 'to steer clear of benefits matters as we already have welfare rights workers' was very potent and that this had come from the team leader, Vernon. So we had a situation where a positive start to integrating social work with a developing awareness of poverty issues and practical benefits knowledge was 'strangled at birth' by the pervasive influence of the team leaders' opposition to involvement with the DSS.

Prior to the establishment of the Social Fund, welfare rights staff spent a great deal of time putting together a comprehensive training course for team leaders over a three day period. It was here that we found indifference and absence from some team leaders (Silverton). Other team leaders were enthusiastic and eager to gain information to pass on to colleagues at team level. I feel that team leaders' advice to social workers not to 'co-operate with the DSS' has been harmful to the so called 'generic' and 'holistic' approach to the point that now team members positively steer clear of benefits related issues and indeed are fearful of becoming entangled in the system for fear of being exposed as de-skilled in this area. We have referrals for such routine matters as the completion of benefit claim forms.

I suggest:

a) More specialist welfare rights staff attached to social work teams.

b) Take the income maintenance issues, and associated stress away from social workers and place more emphasis on a knowledge of the social security system and a strengthened 'advocacy' approach.

c) I think poverty awareness training is essential coupled with more benefits system training at the social work student stage (which is now the case).

d) I would also like to see more use of the direct client - social services relationship for benefits take-up work.

e) I feel some knowledge of the DSS system of 'out of hours' emergency payments scheme may have helped to (the DSS social fund officer comes out to the clients' home now with cash!) avert the use of S17 funds.

Monica, I really enjoyed reading your paper and fieldwork conclusions. I'm sorry that our contact rather faded towards the end owing to my disappearance underneath a mountain of casework. I should like perhaps sometime in the future to use your paper as a basis for discussion with the Team about attitudes, approach and further training.

Your work was really valuable and I'd appreciate any feedback from other sources you receive.

With best regards

Brian Lunt

Bibliography

Abell, N. and McDonnel, J. (1990), 'Preparing for Practice: Motivations, Expectations and Aspirations of the MSW class of 1990', *Journal of Social Work Education*, 26, 1, Winter, 57-64.
Ajzen, I. and Fishbein, M. (1977), 'Attitude Behaviour Relations: A Theoretical Analysis and Review of Empirical Research', *Psychological Bulletin*, 84, pp. 888-918.
Ajzen, I. and Fishbein, M. (1980), *Understanding Attitudes and Predicting Social Behaviour*, Prentice Hall: Englewood-Cliffs, N.J.
Ajzen, I. and Madden, T. (1986), 'Prediction of Goal-Directed Behaviour: Attitudes, Intentions, and Perceived Behavioural Control', *Journal of Experimental Social Psychology*, Vol.32, p. 453-474.
Alcock, P. (1991a), 'The End of the Line for Social Security: the Thatcherite Restructuring of Welfare', *Critical Social Policy*, Spring, pp. 334-348.
Alcock, P., Shepherd, J. and Stewart, G. (1991b), 'Welfare Rights Work into the 1990's - a Changing Agenda', *Journal of Social Policy*, Vol.20, Part 1, January, pp. 41-63.
Archbishop of Canterbury's Commission on Urban Priority Areas, (1986), *Faith in the City*, Church House.
ATD Fourth World (1996) *Talk With Us, Not At Us*, ATD Fourth World: Paris, London.
Bagozzi, R. (1992), 'The Self Regulation of Attitudes, Intentions and Behaviour', *Social Psychology Quarterly*. Vol. 55, No. 2, pp. 178-204.
Balloch, S. and Jones, B. (1990), *Poverty and Anti-Poverty Strategy: The Local Government Response*, Association of Metropolitan Authorities: London.
Bandura, A., Adams, N. and Beyer, J. (1977), 'Cognitive Processes Mediating Behavioural Change', *Journal of Personality and Social Psychology*, 35,

pp. 125-139.
Bandura, A., Adams, N., Hardy, A. and Howells, G. (1980), 'Tests of the Generality of Self-Efficacy Theory', *Cognitive Therapy and Research*, 4, pp. 39-66.
Barbour, R. (1984), 'Social Work Education : Tackling the Theory - Practice Dilemma', *British Journal of Social Work*, 14, pp. 557-777.
Barclay, P. (1982), 'A New Direction for Social Work - The Barclay Report and its Implications', *Community Care*, 1 February, p. 7.
Barclay Report (1982), *Social Workers : Their Role and Tasks*, Bedford Square Press: London.
Barry, K. (1989), 'Biography and the Search for Women's Subjectivity', *Women Studies International Forum*, Vol.12, No.6, pp. 318-331.
Bastin, R. (1985), 'Participant Observation in Social Analysis', in Walker, R. *Applied Qualitative Research*, Gower: Aldershot
Becker, H. (1966), *Outsiders*, Free Press: New York.
Becker, S. (1987), *Social Workers' Attitudes to Poverty and the Poor*, PhD Thesis, University of Nottingham.
Becker, S. and MacPherson, S. (eds) (1988), *Public Issues Private Pain*, Social Services Insight Books: London.
Becker, S. (1991), *Windows of Opportunity: Public Policy and the Poor*, CPAG: London.
Becker, S. and Silburn, R. (1991) *The New Poor Clients : Social Work, Poverty and the Social Fund*, Community Care and Benefits Research Unit, University of Nottingham.
Becker S. (1997), *Responding to Poverty*, Longman: Harlow.
Bell, C. and Encell, S. (1976), (eds) *Inside the Whale*, Pergamon: London and New York.
Bennett, T. and Oppenheim, C. (1991) 'Welfare for the Rich or Poor?' *Poverty Journal*, pp. 32-34, CPAG: London.
Beresford, P. and Croft, S. (1993), 'Community Care and Citizenship in Open University Workbook 3, *Community Care*, Open University: Milton Keynes.
Berger, P. and Luckman, T. (1967), *The Social Construction of Reality*, Penguin: Harmondsworth.
Berthoud, R. and Kempson, E. (1990), *Credit and Debt in Britain: First Findings*, Policy Studies Institute: London.
Beveridge, W. (1909 & 1930), *Unemployment: A Problem of Industry*, Longmans Green and Co.: London.
Beveridge, W. (1942), *Social Insurance and Allied Services*, HMSO, Cmnd. 6404, reprinted 1984.
Biesteck, F. (1961), *The Casework Relationship*, Unwin: London
Bradley, G. and Manthorpe, J. (1997), *Dilemmas of Financial Assessment*,

Venture Press: Birmingham.

Bradshaw, J. (1988), *Lone Parents: Policy in the Doldrums*, Family Policy Studies Centre: London.

Bradshaw, J. and Holmes, H. (1989), *Living on the Edge - A Study of the Living Standards of Families on Benefit in Tyne and Wear*, CPAG: London.

Brady, J. (1987), *Living in Debt*, Birmingham Settlement Money Advice Centre: Birmingham.

Bryson, A. (1991), in Burrows, R. (ed.), *Deciphering the Enterprise Culture*, Routledge: London.

Burgess, R. (1988), *Studies in Qualitative Methodology*, JAI Press: Greenwich, Conn.

Campfens, H. (1992) 'The New Reality of Poverty and Social Work Interventions' in *International Social Work*, April, Vol. 35, No. 2, pp. 99-104.

Cannan, C. (1975), 'Welfare Rights and Wrongs' in Bailey, R. and Brake, M. (eds) *Radical Social Work*, Edward Arnold: London.

Caplan, A. (1998) cited in 'The Happy Hundreds?' article by Dobson, R. *The Guardian* 17/2/98.

Castaneda, C. (1973), *Tales of Power*, Penguin: Harmondsworth.

CCETSW, (1988), *Survey of Social Workers Attitudes to their Training*, Central Council for Education and Training in Social Work: London.

CCETSW, (1989), *Welfare Rights in Social Work Education*, (ed.) Stewart, J. Paper 28.1 CCETSW: London.

CCETSW, (1991), *Rules and Requirements for the Diploma in Social Work. DipSW*, CCETSW: London.

Citizens Advice Bureau (1998) *New Ambitions for Our Country : A New Contract for Welfare*. A CAB response to the Government's Green Paper. July, National Association of Citizens Advice Bureaux: London.

Cochrane, A. and Clarke, J. (1993), *Comparing Welfare States*, Sage: London.

Cohen, R. and Rushton, A. (1982), *Welfare Rights*, Heinemann: London.

Cook, D. (1989), *Rich Law Poor Law*, Open University Press: Milton Keynes.

Cook, S. and Sellitz, (1964), 'A Multiple Indicator Approach to Attitude Measurement' in Warren, N. and Jahoda, M. (eds), *Attitudes*, Penguin: Harmondsworth.

Cooper, S. (1985), *Observations in Supplementary Benefit Offices*, The Reform of Supplementary Benefit Working Paper C, Policy Studies Institute: London.

Craig, G. and Coxall, J. (1989), *Monitoring the Social Fund. A Bibliography 1985-9*, University of Bradford.

Currie, H. and Davidson, R. (1984) *Social Workers, Clients and Financial*

Problems, Research Report commissioned by the Social Work Services Group of the Scottish Education Department.
Davidson, R. and Erskine, A (eds) (1992) *Poverty, Deprivation and Social Work*. Jessica Kingsley: London.
Davies, M. (1994), *The Essential Social Worker*, Arena: London.
Davies G. and Piauchaud D. (1983) 'Social Policy and the Economy' in Glennerster, H. *The Future of the Welfare State*, Heinemann: London.
Davies, M. and Wright, A. (1989), *Probation Training : Consumer Perspective*, Research Report 1, Norwich, University of Anglia, Social Work. Norwich.
Davis, A. and Brook, E. (1985), *Women, The Family and Social Work*, Tavistock: London.
Davis, A., Grimwood, C. and Stewart, G. (1987) 'The Benefits of Benefits Training', *Community Care*, 12/3, pp. 30-31.
De Almeida, P. (1980), 'A Review of Group Discussion Methodology'. *European Research*, Vol 8, Part 3, pp. 114-120.
De Schweinitz, K. (1961), *England's Road to Social Security*, Barnes: New York.
Dean, M. (1991), *The Constitution of Poverty*, Routledge: London.
Dean, R. and Fleck, H. (1992) 'Teaching Clinical Theory and Practice through a Constructivist Lens' *Journal of Teaching in Social Work*, 6 , 1, pp. 3-20.
Denzin, N.K. (1970), *The Research Act in Sociology: A Theoretical Introduction to Sociological Methods*, Butterworths: London.
Department of Education, (1988), *Education Reform Act*, HMSO: London.
Department of Education, (1990), *Education No 2 Act, 1986*, HMSO: London.
Department of Employment, (1990) *Unemployment Benefit Form*, (UB40) HMSO: London.
Department of Health, (1989), *Caring for People*, CM288, HMSO: London.
Department of Health, (1990), *NHS Reforms and You*, Ref.HSR6, HMSO: London.
Department of Health (1990), *Community Care in the Next Decade and Beyond*. HMSO: London.
Department of Health (1997), *Community Care (Direct Payments) Act 1996. Policy and Practice Guideline*, HMSO: London.
DSS, (1995), *Social Security Statistics 1994*, HMSO: London.
Dollard, J. (1949), 'Under What Conditions do Opinions Predict Behaviour', *Public Opinion Quarterly*, Vol.12, pp. 235-65.
Dominelli, L. (1988), 'Thatcher's Attack on Social Security : Restructuring Social Control', *Critical Social Policy*, Issue 23, Autumn, pp. 32-45.
Dominelli, L. (1991), *Women Across Continents : Feminist Comparative Social Policy*, Harvester Wheatsheaf: Hemel Hempstead.
Donnison, D. (1955), 'Observations on University Training For Social Work

in Great Britain and North America', *Social Services Review*, December, pp. 71-81.

Dowling, M. (1986), *Social Work Students' Knowledge and Understanding of the Supplementary Benefit System*, unpublished M.Phil Thesis, University of Hertfordshire.

Dowling, M. (1993), 'The Restructuring of Welfare - What's in it for Social Service Users?'in Page, R. and Deakin, N. (eds) *The Costs of Welfare*, Avebury: Aldershot.

Dowling, M. (1995, 1996, 1997), *Seven Qualitative Reports with Social Service Users and Carers -Older People, People with Physical Disabilities, People with Mental Health Difficulties, Children and Families, People with Learning Disabilities -Their Experiences of Community Care*, Surrey Social Services Department and Royal Holloway, University of London.

Drakeford, M. (1998), 'Poverty and Community Care', Chapter 16 in Symonds, A. and Kelly, A. (Eds) *The Social Construction of Community Care*, Macmillan: London.

Edwards, D. and Potter, J. (1992), *Discursive Psychology*, Sage: London.

Edwards, P. (1983), 'The Sharp End of Bias', *Network*, No.27, October, p.136.

EEC Statistics, (1991), as quoted in *New Internationalist*, June, p. 37.

Entwistle, N. (1987), 'A Model of the Teaching - Learning Process Derived from Research on Student Learning', in Richardson, J., Eysenck, M. and Warren Piper, D. (eds.), *Student Learning : Research in Education and Cognitive Psychology*, RSRHE and Open University: Milton Keynes.

Fabricant, M. and Burghardt, S. (1992), *The Welfare State Crisis and the Transformation of Social Service Work*, M.E.Sharpe Inc.: London.

Family Budget Unit, (1995), *'Modest but Adequate': Summary Budgets for Sixteen Households, October 1994 Prices*, Family Budget Unit: London.

Family Welfare Association, (1990), 'Charities, The Social Fund and Income Support', *Benefits Research*, April, pp. 34- 36.

Fimister, G. (1986), *Welfare Rights Work in Social Services*, Macmillan: Basingstoke.

Fimister, G. (1988), 'The Organisation of Welfare Rights Work in Social Services' in MacPherson, S. and Becker, S. (eds), *Public Issues, Private Pain*, Insight: London.

Finch, J. and Groves, D. (eds.), (1983), *A Labour of Love: Women, Work and Caring*, Routledge and Kegan Paul: London.

Fishbein, M. (1967), 'Attitude and the Prediction of Behaviour', in M, Fishbein, (ed.), *Readings in Attitude Theory and Measurement*, Wiley: New York.

Ford, J. (1990), 'Households, Housing and Debt', *Social Studies Review*, May, pp. 341-354.

Ford, J. (1991), *Consuming Credit, Debt and Poverty in the UK*, CPAG: London.
Ford, J. (1995), *Which Way out? Borrowers with Long Term Mortgage Arrears*, Shelter: London.
Ford, J. and Wilcox, S. (1992), *Reducing Mortgage Arrears and Possessions: An Evaluation of the Initiatives*, Joseph Rowntree Foundation: York.
France, A. (1995), *Youth and Citizenship in the 1990's : An Ethnography of Life in Westhill*. Unpublished PhD, University of Sheffield.
Freed, A. (1995), 'Social Services and Social Work Education' *International Social Work* 38, 1, Jan, pp. 39-51.
Friedman, M. and Friedman, R. (1980), *Free to Choose : A Personal Statement*, Harcourt Brace, Javanovich: New York.
Galbraith, J.K. (1996), *The Good Society*, Sinclair-Stevenson: London.
Gallup Poll, (1981), as cited in New Society 15/7, pp. 37-41.
Gardiner, D. (1988), 'Improving Students' Learning - Setting an Agenda for Quality in the 1990's', *Issues in Social Work Education*, 8, 1, pp. 3-10.
Gardiner, D. (1989), *The Anatomy of Supervision - Developing Learning and Practice Competence for Social Work Students*, Open University Press: Milton Keynes.
Gardiner, D. and Mathias, P. (1988), 'Improving Learning: The Impact of Learning on Professional Training and Staff Development Programmes', *Aspects of Educational Technology : Proceedings of ETIC*, Kogan Page.
Giddens, A. (1998), *The Third Way*. Polity Press: Oxford.
Glendinning, C. and Millar, J. (eds.), (1992), *Women and Poverty in Britain, The 1990's* Wheatsheaf: London and New York.
Goffman, E. (1990), *Stigma : Notes on the Management of Spoiled Identity*, Penguin: Harmondsworth.
Gregory, L. (1991), *Social Services Departments and One Parent Families*, unpublished M.Phil Thesis, University of Sheffield.
Griffiths, R. (1988), *Community Care: Agenda for Action*, HMSO: London.
Guttman, D. and Cohen, B. (1992) 'Teaching about Poverty in Israeli Schools of Social Work', *International Social Work*, Vol. 35, No. 1, pp. 49-63.
Harris, R. (1972), 'Prejudice and Tolerance', cited by Gallagher, A. (1989), *Human Relations*, Vol.42, p. 917.
Harrison, P. (1983), *Inside the Inner City*, Penguin: Harmondsworth.
Harvey, D. (1988), *Lecture to ESRC Postgraduate Students at the School for Advanced Urban Studies*, University of Bristol.
Hedges, A. (1985), 'Group Interviewing' in Walker, R. (ed.), *Applied Qualitative Research*, pp. 71-92, Gower: Aldershot.
Hill, M., Tolan, F. assisted by Smith, R. (1984), *Impact of Changes in the Supplementary Benefits system upon Local Authority Social Services Departments*, School of Advanced Urban Studies, University of Bristol,

(unpublished).
Hill, M. and Laing, P. (1979), *Social Work and Money*, Allen and Unwin: London.
Hill, M. (1990), *Social Security Policy in Britain*, Edward Elgar: Aldershot.
Hirsch, D. (1998), 'Who's Better Off Under Labour?' *New Statesman*, 25/9, pp. 18-20.
Hirst, P. (1998), 'Social Welfare and Associative Democracy', in Ellison, N. and Pierson, C. (Eds) *Developments in British Social Policy*, pp. 78-91, Macmillan: Basingstoke.
Holdaway, S. (1982), 'An Inside Job: A Case Study of Covert Research on the Police', p. 59-79, in M. Bulmer (ed.), *Social Research Ethics*, Macmillan: Basingstoke.
Holman, R. (1973a), 'Poverty, welfare rights and social work', *British Journal of Social Work*, Vol 4, No. 12, 6 September, pp. 358-363.
Holman, R. (1973b), 'Poverty : Consensus and Alternatives' in Fitzgerald, M. et al (eds), *Welfare in Action*, R & KP: London.
Howe, D. (1989), 'Evaluating Social Work Training and Education', *Issues in Social Work Education*, Vol.9, No's. 1, 2, pp. 3-20.
Huby, M. and Dix, G. (1992) *Evaluating the Social Fund*, HMSO: London.
Hudson, A. (1989), 'Changing Perspectives: Feminism, Gender and Social Work' in Langan, M. and Lee, P. *Radical Social Work Today*, Unwin Hyman: London.
International Movement ATD Fourth World, (1991), 'The Wresinski Approach : The Poorest Partners in Democracy', cited in *Poverty Journal*, CPAG, July, pp. 31-35.
Johnson, J. (1975), *Doing Field Research*, Free Press: New York.
Johnson, N. (1990), *Reconstructing the Welfare State, 1980-1990*, Harvester Wheatsheaf: Hemel Hempstead.
Johnson, P. and Webb, S. (1991), *UK Poverty Statistics : A Comparative Study*, Institute for Fiscal Studies, Commentary No. 27: London.
Jones, B. (1989), 'Section One: At the Crossroads', *Benefits Research*, Vol. 3, pp. 22-25.
Jordan, B. (1987), 'Counselling, Advocacy and Negotiation', *British Journal of Social Work*, 17, pp. 169-186.
Jordan, B. (1990), *Social Work in an Unjust Society*, Harvester Wheatsheaf: Hemel Hempstead.
Jordan, B., James, S., Kay, H. and Redley, M. (1992), *Trapped in Poverty? Labour-Market Decisions in Low Income Households*, Routledge: London.
Kelly, A. (1991), 'The Enterprise Culture and the Welfare State : Restructuring the Management of the Health and Personal Social Services', in Burrows, R. (ed.), (1991), *Deciphering the Enterprise Culture*, Routledge: London.
Kingsley, S. (1985), *Action Research Method or Ideology?*, Association of

Researchers in Voluntary Action and Community Involvement, Occasional Paper No.8. London.
Lakatos, I. (1970), 'Falsification and the Methodology of Scientific Research Programmes', in Lakatos, I. and Musgrave, A. (eds.), *Criticism and the Growth of Knowledge*, Cambridge University Press: London.
Langan, M. and Lee, P. (eds.), (1989), *Radical Social Work Today*, Unwin Hyman: London.
Langan, M. (1993), 'New Directions in Social Work' in Clarke, J. (ed.), *A Crisis in Care?*, Sage: London.
Larochelle, C. and Campfens, H. (1992) 'The Structure of Poverty: A Challenge for the Training of Social Workers in the North and South', *International Social Work*, Vol. 35, No. 2, pp. 105-119.
Laws, S. (1991), 'Women on the Verge', *Trouble and Strife*, Spring, pp. 23-25.
Leaper, B. (1988), 'Cash and Care in a European Perspective' in Becker, S. and MacPherson, S. (eds.), *Public Issues, Private Pain*, Insight: London.
Le Grand, J. (1982), *The Strategy of Equality*, Allen & Unwin: London.
Le Grand J. (1997), 'Knights, Knaves or Pawns? Human Behaviour and Social Policy' *Journal of Social Policy*, 26, 2, pp. 149-169.
Lewis, O. (1966), 'The Culture of Poverty', *Scientific American*, 215 : 4, pp.19-25.
Liddell, A. (1989), 'Working for Patients : A Blue Print for the 1990's', *Public Money and Management*, Summer, pp. 131-139.
Lister, R. and Emmett, T. (1976), *Under the Safety Net*, Poverty Pamphlet 25, CPAG: London.
Lister, R. (1988), *The Politics of Social Security : An Assessment of the Fowler Review*, University of Bradford.
Lister, R. (1990a), *The Exclusive Society. Citizenship and the Poor*, CPAG: London.
Lister, R. (1990b), *The Politics of Child Poverty : Reflections on Three Decades*, unpublished paper, University of Bradford.
Lister, R., and Beresford, P. (1991), *Working Together Against Poverty*, Open Services Project and University of Bradford.
Lister, R. (1998), 'Citizenship on the Margins : Citizenship, Social Work and Social Action', *European Journal of Social Work*, Vol. 1, No. 1, pp. 5-18.
Lord, S. and Kennedy, E. (1992), 'Intervening in Poverty at the Grassroots Level : A School-Community Partnership in the United States', *International Social Work*, Vol. 35, No. 2, pp. 255-266.
Lyons, K. (1992), 'An NGO's response to poverty and powerlessness on a British Housing estate: implications for social work education' *International Social Work* 35(2), pp. 243-53.
Malpass, P. (1998), 'Housing Policy', in Ellison, N. and Pierson, C. (Eds)

Developments in British Social Policy, Macmillan: London.

Manstead, A., Proffitt, C. and Smart, J. (1983), 'Predicting and Understanding Mothers, Infant Feeding Intentions and Behaviour : Testing the Theory of Reasoned Action', *Journal of Personality and Social Psychology*, 44, pp.657-671.

Mack, J. and Lansley, S. (1985), *Poor Britain*, Allen and Unwin: London.

Mathinson, J. and Sinclair, I. (1979), *Mate and Stalemate*, Blackwell.

Mayer, J. and Timms, N. (1970), *The Client Speaks*, Routledge & Kegan Paul: London.

McBroom, W. and Reed, F. (1992), 'Towards a Reconceptualisation of Attitude-Behaviour Consistency', *Social Psychology Quarterly*. Vol. 55, No. 2, pp. 205-216.

McCormick, J. and Oppenheim, C. (1998), *Welfare in Working Order*, Institute for Public Policy Research: London.

McGrail, S. (1983), *Survey into the Teaching of Welfare Rights on Postgraduate CQSW Courses in the United Kingdom*, Department of Sociology, University of Stirling.

McKay, A. (1998), 'Social Security Policy in Britain', in Ellison, N. and Pierson, C. (Eds) *Developments in British Social Policy*. Macmillan: Basingstoke.

Means, R. and Smith R. (1994), *Community Care, Policy and Practice*, Macmillan: Basingstoke.

Millar, J. (1992), 'Lone Mothers and Poverty' in Glendinning, C. and Millar, J. (eds.), *Women and Poverty in Britain, The 1990's* Harvester Wheatsheaf: London.

Mills, C.W. (1970), *The Sociological Imagination*, Penguin: Harmondsworth.

Mishra, R. (1984), *The Welfare State in Crisis*, Wheatsheaf: Brighton.

Morgan, D. (1981), 'Men, Masculinity and the Process of Sociological Enquiry', in Roberts, H., *Doing Feminist Research*, Routledge and Kegan Paul: London.

Morris, L. (1984), 'Redundancy and Patterns of Household Finance', *The Sociological Review*, New Series, Vol.32, No.3.

Morris, J. (1994), *The Shape of Things to Come? User-led Social Services*, Social Services Policy Forum Paper No 3, NISW: London.

Munday, B. and Ely, P. (1996) *Social Care in Europe*. Prentice Hall: Hemel Hempstead.

Murray, C. (1990), *The Emerging British Underclass*, Institute of Economic Affairs: London.

National Institute for Social Work (1998) *Report on the Responses to Department of Health consultation on postgraduate social workers*. NISW: London.

National Policy Forum (1998), *National Policy Forum: Report to Conference*.

Labour Party: London.
Noble, M. and Stewart, G. (1987), *Welfare Rights and Social Work Education, Report of CCETSW Conference 6/4/87 on Teaching Welfare Rights*, CCETSW: London.
Norman, P. and Smith, L. (1995), 'The Theory of Planned Behaviour and Exercise : An Investigation into the Role of Prior Behaviour, Behavioural Intentions and Attitude Variability', *European Journal of Social Psychology*, Vol. 12, No. 4, pp. 403-415.
Novak, T. (1988), *Poverty and the State*, Open University Press: Milton Keynes.
Office of Fair Trading, (1989), *Overindebtedness*, HMSO: London.
Oppenheim, C. (1990a), *Holes in the Safety Net*, CPAG: London.
Oppenheim, C. (1991), *Poverty in London : An Overview*, CPAG: London
Oppenheim, C. and Harker, L. (1996), *Poverty The Facts*, 3rd edition CPAG: London.
Packman, J. (1975), *The Child's Generation*, Blackwell: Oxford.
Parker, G. (1987), 'Making Ends Meet : Women, Credit and Debt', in Glendinning, C. and Millar, J. (Eds) *Women and Poverty in Britain* Wheatsheaf: Brighton.
Parker, H. (1974), *View from the Boys* David and Charles: Newton Abbot.
Parker, H and Sutherland, H. (1994) 'Basic Income 1994 : Redistributive Effects of transitional BI's', *Citizens' Income Bulletin* Vol. 18, pp. 3-8.
Parsloe, P. and Stevenson, O. (1978), *Social Services Teams : The Practitioner's View*, HMSO: London.
Parsloe, P. (1990), 'Social Work Education in the Year 2000' in *International Social Work*, January, Vol. 33(1), pp. 13-25.
Pearson, G. (1973), 'Social Work as the Privatised Solution of Public Ills', in Fitzgerald et al, (eds) (1977) *Welfare in Action*. Routledge and Kegan Paul: London.
Pearson, G. (1975), 'The Politics of Uncertainty : A Study in the Socialization of the Social Worker', in Jones, H. (Ed) *Towards a New Social Work*, pp. 45-69, Routledge and Kegan Paul: London.
Peponis, R. (1995), *The United Kingdom Mental Health Support Group Movement : Does it Represent the Voice of Individuals with Mental Health Problems?* Occasional paper 1, unpublished.
Piachaud, D. (1987), 'The Growth of Poverty', in Walker, A. and Walker, C. (eds.), *The Growing Divide : A Social Audit 1979-1987*, CPAG: London.
Piachaud, D. (1998), 'Million More Face Poverty Under Labour'. *The Guardian*, 5/1/98.
Pile, H. and O'Donnell, C. (1997), 'Earnings, Taxation and Wealth' in Walker A, and Walker, C. (eds) (1997) *Britain Divided: The Growth of Social Exclusion in the 1980's and 1990's*, CPAG: London.

Pithouse, A. (1987), *Social Work : The Social Organisation of an Invisible Trade*, Avebury : Aldershot.

Polakow, V. (1994), 'Welfare Reform and the Assault on Daily Life : Targeting Single Mothers and Their Children'. *Social Justice*, Spring, Vol. 211(55) pp. 27-32.

Pond, C. (1989), 'The Changing Distribution of Income, Wealth and Poverty' in, Hamnett, C., Mcdowell, L. and Satre, P. *The Changing Social Structure* Sage and Open University Press: London.

Pound, J. (1971), *Poverty and Vagrancy in Tudor England*, Longman: Harlow.

Quiroz, T. (1992), 'Social Policies and the Role of Social Work for the New Times', *International Social Work*, Vol. 35, No. 2, pp. 121-133.

Roberts, H. (ed.), (1990), *Doing Feminist Research*, Routledge and Kegan Paul: London.

Robson, S. (1988), *Group Discussion, Advanced Workshop in Applied Qualitative Research*, SCPR: London.

Rustomfram, N. (1991), 'Training for Communication Skills - Implications for Community Education', *Indian Journal of Social Work*, July, Vol. 52, 3, pp. 303-312.

Ryan, M. (1992), 'Consumer Credit, Debt Poverty and Counselling : The Australian Experience'. *International Social Work*, Vol. 35, No. 2, pp. 217-227.

Sainsbury, E. (1975), *Social Work With Families*, Routledge and Kegan Paul: London.

Satyamurti, C. (1981), *Occupational Survival, The Case of the Local Authority Social Worker*, Blackwell: Oxford.

Schifter, D. and Ajzen, I. (1985), 'Intention, Perceived Control and Weight Loss: An Application of the Theory of Planned Behaviour', *Journal of Personality and Social Psychology*, 49, pp. 843-851.

Schwartz, S. and Robinson, M. (1991), 'Attitudes towards Poverty during Undergraduate Education', *Journal of Social Work Education*, Vol. 27, No. 3, pp. 290-296.

Shanks, N. and Smith, S. (1992), 'Public Policy and the Health of Homeless People' *Policy and Politics* Vol 20, No 1, pp. 35- 46.

Shirley, I. (1990), 'New Zealand : The Advance of the New Right', in Taylor, I., *The Social Effects of Free Market Policies*, Harvester Wheatsheaf: London.

Smart, C. and Smart, B. (eds.), (1978), *Women, Sexuality and Social Control*, Routledge and Kegan Paul: London.

Smith, G. and Harris, R. (1979), 'Ideologies and the Organisation of Social Work Departments', *British Journal of Social Work*, Vol.2, No.1, pp.27-45.

Smith, G. (1980), *Social Need*, Routledge and Kegan Paul: London.

Smith, S. (1988), Lecture on *Philosophy, Methodology and Empirical Research*, ESRC Conference, Quorn Hall, Leicestershire.
Spencer, G. (1982), 'Methodological Issues in the study of Bureaucratic Elites; A Case Study of West Point', pp. 23-31 in Burgess, R. (ed.), *Field Research: A Sourcebook and Field Manual*, Allen and Unwin: London.
Stark, T. (1986), *The A-Z of Wealth*, The Fabian Society: London.
Statham, D. (1978), *Radicals in Social Work*, R & KP: London.
Stevenson, O. (1973), *Claimant or Client?*, Allen and Unwin: London.
Stewart, G. and Stewart, J. (1986), *Boundary Changes : Social Work & Social Security*, CPAG & BASW: London.
Stewart, G. and Stewart, J. (1988), *The Beginning of the End? Welfare Rights Workers' Experience of the Amended Single Payment Regulations*, Cleveland County Welfare Rights Service for WROG, Middlesborough.
Stewart, G. and Stewart, J. (1991), *Relieving Poverty : Use of the Social Fund by Social Work Clients and Other Agencies*, AMA: Birmingham.
Stewart, J. (ed.), (1989), *Welfare Rights in Social Work Education*, Paper 28.1, CCETSW: London.
Taback, R. and Triegaardt, J. (1992), 'Educating Social Workers to Practice in Rural South Africa : Dilemmas and Challenges - A Case Study', *Maatskaplike-Werk/Social Work*, Vol. 28, No. 4, pp. 9-94.
Taylor, I. (ed) (1990), *The Social Effects of Free Market Policies*, Harvester Wheatsheaf: London
Taylor Gooby, P. and Papadakis, E. (1985), 'Who Wants the Welfare State?', *New Society*, 19/7, pp. 23-34.
Timmins, N. (1988), 'A Harsh Way to End the Dependency Culture', *The Independent*, 6/4, p.7.
Titmuss, R. (1958), *Essays on the Welfare State*, Allen and Unwin: London.
Titmuss, R. (1968), *Commitment to Welfare*, Allen and Unwin: London.
Titterton, M. (1986), *Social Explanation, Causal Mechanism and the Epidemiology of Personal and Social Problems*, Social Work Research Centre, University of Stirling, Scotland.
Todaro, M. (1994), *Economic Development*, Longman: New York.
Townsend, P. (1970), *The Concept of Poverty*, Heinemann: London.
Townsend, P. (1979), *Poverty in the United Kingdom : A Survey of Household Resources and Standards of Living*, Penguin: Harmondsworth.
Townsend, P. (1991), *Meaningful Statistics on Poverty 1991*, Statistical Monitoring Unit, University of Bristol.
Tully, G.J. (1994), *Level of Moral Reasoning and Background Factors as Predictors of BSW Students' Interest in Working with People in Poverty*, PhD, New York University.
Tunnard, J. (1973), 'Marriage Breakdown and the Loss of the Owner Occupied Home', *Roof*, Vol.1, No.2, pp. 15-21.

Valencia, M. and Jackson, M. (1979), 'Variation in Provision of Financial Aid through Social Work', *Policy and Politics*, Vol. 7, No. 1, pp. 31-37.
Van Parijs, P. (1992), *Arguing for Basic Income : Ethical Foundations for a Radical Reform*, Verso: London and New York.
Vinton, L. and White, B. (1995), 'The "Boutique Effect" in Graduate Social Work Education'. *Journal of Teaching in Social Work*, Vol. 11, No. 1,2, pp. 3-13.
Walker, A. and Walker, C. (eds) (1997), *Britain Divided The Growth of Social Exclusion in the 1980's and 1990's*, CPAG: London.
Walker, A. (1990), 'The Strategy of Inequality', in Taylor, I. (ed.), *The Social Effects of Free Market Policies*, Harvester Wheatsheaf: London.
Walker, A. (1991), 'The Persistence of Poverty under Welfare States and the Prospect for its Abolition', *International Journal of Health Services*. Vol. 32, No. 3, pp. 21-29.
Walker, R. (1985), (ed.), *Applied Qualitative Research*, Gower: Aldershot
Waxman, C. (1988), *The Stigma of Poverty*, Pergamon: New York.
Weir, J. (1981), 'What do Social Workers do?', *New Society*, 17/5, pp. 17-21.
Whyte, W. F. (1984) *Learning from the Field : A Guide from Experience*, Sage: London.
Wicker, A. (1973), 'Attitudes v Actions: the Relationship of Verbal and Overt Responses to Attitude Objects', in Warren, N. and Jahoda, M. (eds.), (1979), *Attitudes*, Penguin: Harmondsworth.
Williams, F. (1989), *Social Policy, A Critical Introduction*, Polity: Cambridge.
Willis, P. (1993), *Learning to Labour*, Ashgate: Aldershot.
Wilson, G. (1993), 'Users and Providers: Different Perspectives on Community Care Services', *Journal of Social Policy*, Vol. 22, No. 4, pp. 507-526.
Wilson, G. (1995), *Community Care, Asking the Users*, Chapman and Hall: London.
Wilson, W. (1988), 'Academic Controversy and Intellectual Growth', in Riley, M. (ed.), *Sociological Lives*, Sage: Newbury Park, California.

Index

action research 45
advocacy 1, 10, 16, 19, 22, 44, 84,
　　96, 121, 165

BASW 16, 151
Becker, S. 65
benefits 21, 27, 96
behavioural control 101-103, 119,
　　121-122, 142-143, 162
Beveridge, W. 12

carers 25, 126-127, 133, 135, 143,
　　149, 154, 156, 159
　older people 157
　research 143
casework model 5, 11, 14, 19, 20,
　　25, 93
CCETSW 10, 11, 13, 69, 76
CDP (Community Development Projects) 19
Children and Young Persons Act (1963) 15
　(1989) 16, 21
community care 24, 157-162
　grants 16, 21, 23, 89, 107, 122, 138
COS (Charity Organisation Society) 11,
　　12, 13, 14, 21
council housing 27, 35, 40, 42-43
community Care Assessments 24
community Care Grants 16, 21, 23, 89
council Housing 27, 35, 40, 42, 43
CPAG (Child Poverty Action Group) 67,
　　106, 151
crisis care 42

Denzin, N.K. 51
deprivation
　emotional 80
　indicators 6
Direct Cash Payments 1, 21, 24, 117,
　　154

Direct Payments Act (1996) 155
disabled People 9
discrimination 156
DSS 16, 21, 25, 44, 62, 81, 88, 91,
　　92, 107, 111, 113, 126
DSS Tribunal 96

emancipation 48
emancipatory interests 48-50, 64
equal opportunities 10
ethnographic project 64, 127
ethnography 99

Fabian Society 12
Family Expenditure Survey 5
Family Services Unit 79
field observations 51, 52
fieldwork studies 65

gender interactions 3, 48
group discussions 45, 51, 55, 56,
　　76

Hardie, Keir 12
Hertfordshire University 66
homeless people 43
housing 3, 7, 33, 42, 43, 146
Housing Act (1996) 43
housing associations 42
Howe, D. 68

ideology
　need 116
　poverty 12
income 6
　low 6, 22
　minimum 16, 20
　maintenance 1, 2, 16, 22, 42,
　　107, 150

support 6, 15, 43, 127
inequality 1, 6, 24, 97, 156
inter-subjectivity 54

Johnson, J. 54

Kelly, A. 23, 24
Kingsley, Sue 53
knowledge
  external 67
  internal 67

learning disabilities 42
Le Grand, J. 158, 160, 161, 162
Lewis, Oscar 80
lone mothers 6, 43

Manchester Social Services 19
Maslow's hierarchy of needs 152
mental health 20, 40
mental illness 42, 156
methodological
  concerns 46, 48
  triangulation 2, 51
methodology 45, 50
  feminist 53
  quantitative 64
  qualitative 64
Middlesex University 66
models
  empowerment 139
  social constructionist 98, 113
    118, 120, 121
  social psychological 98, 103,
    113, 119, 120, 121
  task centred 139
mortgages 27, 34, 35, 37, 38, 40

NALGO 16
NHS & Community Care Act (1990) 155
need 20
  ideology 116
NE London University 66

ontological concerns 46

participant observation 45, 64, 65,
  138, 145
poor
  deserving xi, 11, 86, 90, 95, 113,
    115, 117, 118, 119, 120, 135,
    143, 147, 150
  disabled 156
  discriminated 162
  elderly 156
  mentally ill 156

undeserving xi, 11, 12, 86, 90, 95,
  98, 113, 118, 119, 120, 143, 147,
  150
young children 156
Poor Law 11, 15
Poor Law Commission 12
poverty 1, 3, 4, 57, 69, 134
  alleviating poverty 10
  attitudes 90
  awareness 9, 22, 69
  culture 8
  definition 5, 6
  depression 6
  discrimination 24
  ideology 12
  line 5, 7
  measuring 6
  mental and physical health 20
  negative attitude 106, 108
  old age 128
  positive attitude 106
  prevention 11
  relief 11
  social problems 44
  social work 20, 25, 91, 92, 93,
    95
  structural nature 80
  theories 74
  unemployment 16
  welfare rights 20, 62, 76
  women 6, 85
poverty awareness programme 1, 3,
    4, 62, 70, 77, 78, 94, 97, 99,
    150, 164
psychiatry 13, 71

qualitative data 50, 58, 78, 97
quantitative information 51, 97
  method 99

realist perspectives 50
research
  action 53, 61
  behavioural 68
  educational 68, 69
  ethnographic 58
  evaluation 68
  feedback 61-62
  feminist 48
  methods 45, 51
  psychological 100
  qualitative 53, 65, 97
  social 48
Royal Holloway College,
  University of London 164

Section 17 payments 86, 87, 107, 112, 113, 114, 115, 137, 138, 147
Sheffield University 66, 67, 79, 164
Sheffield Hallam University 66, 79
social control 1, 48, 82, 83, 84, 148, 150
social deprivation 24
social exclusion 4, 145, 152-153, 163
Social Exclusion Unit 153
Social Fund 15-16, 25, 21, 43, 44, 62, 65, 83, 89, 93, 96, 106, 116, 122, 123, 128, 133, 134, 138, 141, 149, 155
Social Security Act (1986) 15, 23, 155
Social Service Departments 15, 16, 19, 21, 44, 99, 126, 136
social service users 1, 2, 9, 19, 25, 27, 28, 42, 48, 51, 55, 69-71, 78, 83, 103, 107, 117, 126-127, 148
   dissatisfactions 4, 128
   evaluation of social work 143
   financial difficulties 4, 111
   poverty 2, 101
   research 55, 58
social workers xi, 129, 131, 139
social welfare 10
social work 3, 4, 13, 14, 15, 71
   definitions 9, 53
   poverty 145, 147
   preventative 26
   purpose 10
   roots 11
social work education & training xi, 2, 3, 10, 25, 68, 69, 70, 97, 138, 145, 147, 165
social work knowledge 71, 72, 73
social work practice xi, 74, 78
social work students 1, 2, 51, 56, 58, 63, 66, 68, 69, 72, 73, 75, 76, 78, 80, 94, 96, 103, 147
social workers 5, 9, 15, 16, 23, 27, 56, 61, 69, 83, 89
   actions 103
   advocates/advisers 5, 19
   attitude 1, 108, 109, 138, 140, 143
   attitude to poverty 1, 2, 48, 50, 57, 58, 64, 92, 93, 98, 99, 100, 105, 106, 122, 124
   attitude to users 126, 146, 147
   attitude to welfare rights 124
   awareness of poverty 162
   awareness of welfare rights 124
   casework model 14
   cash and care roles 2
   group discussions 51
   income maintenance 19
   interaction with users 27
   manager/purchaser of care 22
   providers 5
   role 151, 152
Stevenson, O. 15
stigma 1, 8, 9, 12, 13, 25, 135, 143, 150, 156
Sure Start Unit 153

theory
   planned behaviour 101, 121
   reasoned action 100-101, 105
   social construction 3, 105, 114, 125, 147, 162
   sociol/psychological 3, 105, 109, 125, 142, 147
theoretical perspectives 50

underclass 8, 80
unemployment 3, 6
UNISON 16, 151
University of Witwatersrand 93

welfare
   benefits 78, 84, 96, 97, 98, 121, 149
   children 15
   restructuring 3, 27, 28, 42, 146
   welfare rights 2, 3, 10, 11, 19, 22-23, 25, 62, 63, 69, 71, 96, 97, 102, 103, 111, 121, 122, 124, 134, 135, 147
   knowledge 74
   teaching 103
Welfare Rights Adviser 22, 49, 88, 123
Welfare Rights Officer 22, 48
Wright Mills, C. 53